The World's Greatest Mysteries

by
Gerry Brown

HAMLYN

Acknowledgements

The Publishers would like to thank the following for their kind permission to reproduce the photographs:

ALDUS ARCHIVE 69, 87, 103, 133; MARY EVANS PICTURE LIBRARY 59, 83, 94, 98, 121, 159; FORTEAN PICTURE LIBRARY 107, 110; THE KOBAL COLLECTION 46; POPPERFOTO 31, 51,/REUTER 63; REX FEATURES LTD 16, 40 left and right, 116,/SIPA 75, 148; SYNDICATION INTERNATIONAL LTD 16 inset, 9 and inset.

First published in 1989 by Octopus Books Ltd

This edition published in 1990 by
The Hamlyn Publishing Group Limited,
part of Reed International Books

Michelin House
81 Fulham Road
London SW3 6RB

Reprinted 1992, 1994

ISBN 0 600 570 126

Printed in Great Britain by Cox & Wyman Ltd

Frontispiece photographs: a zombie, Doris Stokes
The Cottingley Fairies

The World's Greatest Mysteries

Contents

Chapter One

CRIME & INTRIGUE

Some of the most sinister and upsetting mysteries we have to face are those when people suddenly go missing, for no apparent reason and leaving behind them precious little for investigators to go on. Even more sinister, perhaps, are the methods of occultism and psychic clairvoyance, used either to find missing persons or criminals in hiding, or abused by their practitioners, in order to commit dastardly acts ...

Suzy Lamplugh

On Monday 28 July 1986, Suzy Lamplugh made an entry in her business diary. It read: '12.45. Mr Kipper, 37 Shorrolds Road, O/S'.

For 25-year-old Suzy, the summons to get out of doors and meet a perfect stranger must have been a welcome opportunity to have a break from her busy office routine at Sturgis Estate Agents in Fulham Road, west London, where she had worked for 16 months.

The diary note was a simple shorthand reminder to herself. Suzy, a young, ambitious and hard-working estate agent negotiator, was due to meet a client outside that address at the appointed time. The property – a furnished three-storey terraced house – had come on to the books a few days before. The asking price was £128,000 and a successful sale would have meant a tidy commission bonus for the eager young estate agent.

Suzy had spent a wasteful and frustrating morning taking phone calls from potential clients who just wanted to compare house prices with those of rival estate agents, making her own calls to friends, trying to locate her pocket diary and a postcard she had lost before the previous weekend, and notifying her bank manager about her cheque book which had been misplaced at the same time.

But nothing distracted her from her meeting with Mr Kipper. That appointment seemed like a real sales prospect. Mr Kipper could be a serious potential purchaser.

Just before her lunch break she strode over to the desk of Mark Gurdon, the office manager, and collected the keys to the house in Shorrolds Road. The Ford Fiesta car supplied by her employers was parked just outside the office. It would take only three or four minutes for Suzy to drive to her appointment. The office manager expected Suzy would be gone just long enough to show her potential customer around the property before heading back to the office. She would probably bring back a sandwich to eat at her desk, because she was always keen to be there, ready to answer any calls that might lead to more sales and more commission bonuses.

Suzy took only her purse with her, leaving her handbag behind. Then she left the office and drove away to become the subject of the biggest and most puzzling missing persons mystery which has ever baffled the experts at New Scotland Yard.

Missing estate agent Suzy and (inset) 37 Shorrolds Road.

It was only a few hours before her friends and colleagues at the estate agent's began to become concerned about Suzy's absence. At first Mark Gurdon was simply irritated that Suzy seemed to be taking too much time over her visit to the terraced house. He assumed there might be unforeseen complications with the client, possibly caused by lengthy on-the-spot negotiating over the price for the property. But if that had been the case, she should have returned immediately to the office, where she could have taken advice and hammered out any financial details.

He strolled over to Suzy's desk and checked her diary entry. By late afternoon he had become worried. It was unlike Suzy to take long, unauthorized lunch breaks. He decided to check for himself. With another of Suzy's colleagues he drove round to the vacant property. There was no sign of Suzy or her car. But as the two estate agents prepared to leave Shorrolds Road, next door neighbour 58-year-old unemployed bachelor Harry Riglin asked them: 'Are you looking for the young couple?'

Riglin confirmed that Suzy had indeed been at the house with a young man. He had thought they looked like a nice, prosperous young couple as they stood outside and looked up admiringly at the house. The kind of people he would have liked as neighbours.

Mark Gurdon returned to his office. He checked his file of clients. They had never done business before with a 'Mr Kipper'. The mystery client may have only phoned that morning and by sheer chance Suzy had taken the call; or he may have stepped into the office at any time in the past few days after seeing a property in the window display which had caught his eye.

Gurdon's next call was to Suzy's mother, 54-year-old swimming teacher and slimming counsellor Diana Lamplugh, at her home in East Sheen, a few miles away. Gurdon asked if Suzy had skipped work to have lunch with her mother, but Mrs Lamplugh had not seen her daughter since she had paid a visit to her family the day before.

Increasingly worried, Gurdon then began to phone the casualty departments of local hospitals. He went to Fulham police station to report his young sales agent's disappearance, but couldn't afford the time to wait in the lengthy queue at the desk. He hurried off to an appointment with a client, checked Shorrolds Road again, and returned to his office.

Six hours after Suzy had last been seen, Gurdon phoned Fulham police station and spoke to PC Duncan Parker. Immediately, Missing Person Report FF584/1/54 was filed. Next, an urgent call was made to the home of Detective Inspector Peter Johnstone, the officer on call for emergencies, instructing him to take charge of the investigation.

Detective Inspector Johnstone was, at the time, heading the hunt for the murderer of an elderly London woman who had been raped and strangled the week before. When he heard the first details of Suzy's disappearance, he feared he had another murder case on his hands.

Missing persons reports at London police stations fall into two categories: 'active' and 'inactive'. Inactive files cover those whose overwhelming family, career or financial problems seem to give them some melancholy but logical reason for dropping out of sight, cutting off all contact with those closest to them.

But the case of Suzy Lamplugh definitely fell into the 'active' category. For this was a well-adjusted, normal, happy young woman. She had gone for a lunchtime appointment leaving her handbag behind at her office, obviously expecting to return. There was no apparent reason for Suzy Lamplugh to vanish, unless she had been the victim of foul play.

Johnstone quickly ordered local police officers to go to Suzy's own home – a two-bedroomed flat in Putney – and smash their way in if need be. He wanted to make sure that Suzy had not become unwell that day and had simply gone home to sleep off a sudden bout of illness; or that the missing estate agent had not suddenly lost her heart in a mad moment of passion with the mysterious Mr Kipper and had taken him home with her.

At Suzy's flat there was no sign of her or her flatmate, 25-year-old advertising executive Nick Bryant. He was still at work, unaware of Suzy's disappearance.

In Suzy's neat and orderly bedroom lay the material for a dress; there was a partially completed sleeve beside the sewing machine her mother had lent her. There were no signs of a struggle; nor of any visitors; nor of any empty wardrobes, which might have hinted at Suzy running away.

At the same time, two detectives forced their way into the unoccupied 'House for Sale' in Shorrolds Road. There were no clues there either.

Throughout London, a general alert was flashed to all mobile patrols and beat bobbies to locate Suzy's Ford Fiesta, registration number B396 GAN. A 'grid search' was organized, marking off the immediate vicinity of Shorrolds Road into squares, so that every road and side-street could be checked out for signs of Suzy or her car.

Detectives began to build up a picture of Suzy, her friends, her contacts, her boyfriends, her business associates. They found nothing sinister whatsoever. In fact, the picture they had was of a wholesome, beautiful girl-next-door type, who could have been anyone's daughter, sister or friend.

Suzy was a go-ahead, strong-willed girl, the second oldest child of the Lamplugh family, with an older brother and two younger sisters. She had overcome the handicap dyslexia, the inability to read letters and numbers properly, which also afflicted her mother and her brother and sisters. Sufferers from dyslexia see script and text only as a confusing jumble of letters. With the patient help and support of her father, 55-year-old solicitor Paul Lamplugh, Suzy had learned to read and had successfully passed her exams.

After leaving school, Suzy had trained and qualified as a beautician, and went to work in the floating beauty salon of the *Queen Elizabeth II* luxury cruise ship. On board the liner she was known to her shipmates as 'H', because she insisted on being called by her full name and was constantly telling the crew and passengers that her name was 'Susannah – with an H!'?

She had cruised the world and dreamed of settling down in South Africa with a boyfriend she had met on board, but back on dry land, practical and ambitious Suzy had buckled down to hard work as an estate agent, eventually buying her own £70,000 flat in Putney, just south of the river Thames and near to her parents' home.

Although she had lived independently away from home for six years, she visited her parents regularly. In fact, she had been to see her parents the night before she went missing. Just before she kissed them goodbye, Suzy had summed up her own easy-going vitality. 'Life is for living,' she told them.

Mr Riglin, the neighbour who had seen the young couple viewing the house at Shorrolds Road, was able to give police an accurate description of Suzy as she was last seen: 5ft 6in tall, pretty, medium-built with blond streaked hair, wearing a peach blouse, black jacket and grey skirt with high-heeled shoes.

The detectives grilled Riglin at length about Suzy's companion, the man now known to everyone on the case as 'Mr Kipper'. He was a couple of inches taller than Suzy, aged between 25 and 30. He was handsome, slimly built, clean shaven and looked prosperous and wealthy in his neatly tailored dark business suit.

At home in East Sheen, Suzy's parents were frantic with worry. Her father, Paul, travelled to Fulham, anxious to witness for himself the massive police effort now being mounted to locate his daughter. Meanwhile, Diana Lamplugh waited at home by the telephone, hoping against hope that Suzy would call her. Even a message from a kidnapper demanding a ransom would have been welcome.

Offering what little help he could, Paul Lamplugh joined two detectives in their patrol car and toured the streets of west London, hoping to spot his daughter among the happy crowds of young people sipping drinks in wine bars or queueing for cinema seats. He had only been in the patrol car a few minutes when he heard the radio message announcing the first clue to Suzy's disappearance. The Ford Fiesta car she had driven that day had been found in Stevenage Road, a quiet residential street. It was a little over a mile from the vacant property where Suzy had met Mr Kipper and in the opposite direction from the route she would have taken to return to the office.

By now, it was 10 p.m., and Detective Inspector Johnstone decided that a full forensic examination would have to wait until daylight. In the meantime, careful not to accidentally wipe out any fingerprints or disturb any microscopic hairs or fibres invisible to the naked eye, the police inspected the abandoned car as closely as they dared.

The Ford Fiesta had been parked at a slight angle to the kerb and the rear end of the car was partially blocking the entrance to a garage. It had been dumped there by someone in a hurry; the handbrake had been left in the off position.

The driver's door was unlocked, but the passenger door was firmly secure, suggesting that only one person had been driving the car. On the back shelf they could clearly see Suzy's straw hat.

The police meticulously opened the driver's door and prised up the back shelf to check the boot of the car. It was empty. But in the rack of the door, they found a purse.

Then they found the most intriguing clue of all: the driver's seat, which would normally have been moved forward in the position closest to the steering wheel for a girl like Suzy, had been pushed back several notches. It seemed likely that the car had been driven to its final parking place by someone several inches taller than Suzy; possibly a man; probably Mr Kipper.

There the clues stopped.

Since the disappearance of Suzy Lamplugh there have been reports of her being seen alive in many different locations, from London nightspots to the sun-soaked beaches of Spanish and Greek holiday resorts. The release of a photo-fit impression of the shadowy figure of Mr Kipper produced a flood of calls to the police, but no solid leads.

In the search for Suzy, the biggest ever mounted by New Scotland Yard, more than 26,000 separate index cards were filed on computer, detailing every aspect of Suzy's life and those of her friends, family and almost everyone who had come in contact with her.

In the busy sales offices of estate agents throughout London, worried staff began to change their carefree office routines. Before any male customers were fixed up with appointments with young female negotiators with a prospect of buying property, they were asked to call in at the office where colleagues could discreetly make a note of their description and the number of the vehicle they drove.

Potential buyers making telephone appointments were asked for contact numbers and business addresses, where their identities could be verified before any female negotiator was despatched to meet them.

Nine months after Susannah Jane Lamplugh disappeared with the mysterious Mr Kipper, a remembrance service was held at her family's local church,

All Saints, East Sheen. Everyone who attended wore bright clothes and buttonhole flowers, like at a wedding. It was a celebration of the life of the young estate agent, they were told. They heard of the launch of the Suzy Lamplugh Trust, a charity dedicated to making life safer and less fearful for young career girls.

And they heard Paul Lamplugh say of his daughter: 'While we do not believe that Suzy is alive, we do not believe she is dead. That is the paradox.'

Helen Smith

As a former detective with the Leeds police force in Yorkshire, Ron Smith was no stranger to seeing the bodies of victims of violent death. But he had to steel his courage to near breaking point on the night of Saturday 26 May 1979, when he was led into the mortuary of the Baksh Hospital in Jeddah, Saudi Arabia. The body he had come to view was not that of some faceless stranger – it was the body of his own daughter, Helen.

Ron Smith had been living with the grief of his daughter's death since he had received a phonecall a week earlier telling him that 23-year-old Helen had died tragically in an accident in Jeddah, falling from a balcony of a block of flats where she had gone to a party.

Choking back his emotions, the ex-policeman, now a successful business-man, had flown to the Middle East, where Helen had been working as a nurse since the Baksh Hospital had opened 15 months earlier. He simply wanted to bring her body home for burial.

Sympathetic Foreign Office officials who met him in the Saudi capital could offer him little comfort. In an attempt to explain the circumstances surrounding Helen's death, they escorted him to the local prison to meet Richard Arnot, the English senior surgeon at Baksh Hospital.

Arnot was awaiting trial for breaching the strict Saudi Muslim law banning alcohol. He had hosted the drinks party at which Helen had died.

Arnot could only outline briefly that Helen had died as a result of a fall from the balcony of his sixth-floor flat in the hospital complex. There had been a lot of heavy, illegal drinking at the party and another party guest, a 31-year-old Dutchman, Johannes Otten, had also been killed in a 70-foot tumble from the same balcony. Arnot claimed he had slept through the fatal drama, and knew none of the details.

The distressed father brushed aside diplomatic objections and demanded to see the body of his dead daughter. When mortuary attendant Subi Bakir drew back the shroud over Helen's body, Ron Smith began to have doubts about the authorities' simple explanation for her death. Helen's body showed some signs of internal bleeding but, apart from this, there was no evidence of the massive injuries one would normally expect to see in someone who had crashed from a great height on to the solid concrete forecourt outside the block of flats.

Ron Smith was soon convinced that his daughter's death was not a simple accident, but a bizarre murder mystery. He set out on a dogged crusade of investigation and inquiry which was still unresolved a decade later. In fact, the mystery of his daughter's death may *never* be explained.

The official Saudi police report accepted Helen Smith's death as a tragic accident. But when Ron Smith gave them the results of his own detective work – five days spent interviewing hospital staff who knew the background to the events leading up to Doctor Arnot's wild drinks party – they began to change their minds.

On 2 June, Saudi government pathologist Dr Ali Kheir carried out a detailed post mortem examination on the body. He found no evidence of fractures of the neck, shoulder blades or spine. As Ron Smith prepared to fly home to England, he was assured that police were now treating his daughter's death as a murder enquiry.

A year later, when he had only received evasive answers from the Saudi Government and British Foreign Office diplomats about the progress of the murder investigation, Ron Smith was informed that heavy punishments for the hosts of the party and some of their guests had been ordered by the Serious Crimes Court: three German guests at the party suffered no further penalties; two other Germans were sentenced to 30 lashes each; Richard Arnot was sentenced to a year in prison and 80 lashes for consuming alcohol and allowing his wife Penny to commit adultery with a party guest, New Zealand-born deep sea diver Tim Hayter. Mrs Arnot and Hayter were also sentenced to 80 lashes, to be administered in front of a crowd. But there were no charges against anyone in relation to Helen Smith's death.

After five months in prison, the Arnots and their party friends were all released on bail.

In June 1980, Ron Smith decided his only hope of unravelling the mystery of the fatal drinks party lay in uncovering the facts before a British court. He

15

Dr and Mrs Arnot and (inset) Nurse Helen Smith.

flew to Jeddah, collected his daughter's body and returned to Leeds. There he petitioned acting coroner Mr Miles Coverdale for an inquest.

Coroners can, if they wish, conduct inquests into the death of any British subject anywhere in the world, but Mr Coverdale ruled that the death had taken place outside his jurisdiction and would, therefore, not conduct an inquest. He did, however, agree to carry out his legal obligation to commission an official autopsy, which was carried out by Home Office pathologist Dr Michael Green, at Leeds University. The coroner later announced that the autopsy report confirmed that Helen had suffered injuries consistent with a fall from a height, and an inquest would not be necessary.

But Ron Smith claimed the autopsy report was full of inaccuracies. He found, for instance, references to 'bruises to the face that were consistent with slaps and punches'. He saw this as proof that Helen had been severely beaten, and possibly even murdered, before her body was thrown over the balcony, or placed there by her murderer to make it look as if she and the Dutch guest, Johannes Otten, had both fallen to their deaths.

A month after his report, Dr Green, the pathologist, admitted in a newspaper interview: 'If I was to say Helen Smith's death was an accident, I would be a liar. My conscience would not allow me to say so.'

The interview led to a storm of publicity about the mystery death, and public interest was suddenly aroused. Ron Smith, who had already travelled to Holland to consult the family of Johannes Otten, then hired one of Europe's most respected pathologists to carry out another post mortem.

In December 1980, Danish Professor Jorgen Dalgaard conducted his own autopsy, with Dr Green also present. Professor Dalgaard's report, submitted three months later, uncovered an injury unnoticed until then: a wound covering the whole of the left side of the scalp. He concluded that the wound could have caused bleeding inside the brain leading to Helen falling unconscious or possibly even dying before she sustained any of the other injuries.

It wasn't until March 1982, after a long and bitter legal battle, that two High Court judges ruled that an inquest should be held into Helen's death. The inquest finally opened before a jury in Leeds in November 1982. It was to be a costly hearing, with witnesses flown in from around the world. Dr Richard Arnot, now divorced, had to travel from Australia. His ex-wife, the party hostess Penelope Arnot, announced her marriage to an American journalist and was no longer subject to a subpoena from a British court. And Tim Hayter – another vital witness – did not attend the inquest either.

The evidence of the witnesses at the inquest was a tale of drunkenness and confusion. The party had been organized as a farewell gesture for New Zealander Hayter, who had become a friend of the Arnots' when he had offered to teach the doctor and his wife scuba diving.

At the party there had been five German salvage experts working on a Saudi contract. One German witness said that their hosts, the Arnots, had provided liberal supplies of whisky for the party and had invited Helen because she worked at the hospital with Dr Arnot and often acted as a babysitter for their children. Salvage worker Martin Fleischer testified that they had all helped themselves to large quantities of drink, risking harsh penalties under Saudi law, which strictly prohibits alcohol even for foreign residents and guest workers.

Some time after the party was already under way, Helen arrived and chatted and mingled with the guests. Later still, Doctor Arnot turned up, although his wife had already been acting as a generous hostess.

Dr Arnot went to bed around 2 a.m. leaving his guests to continue the party. Fleischer added that he and his German friends had drifted away shortly afterwards and returned to their digs on board a floating accommodation barge in Jeddah Harbour. When he and his workmates left, Helen and Johannes, Tim Hayter and Mrs Arnot, and a French guest, Jacques Texier, a marine biologist, were still drinking and enjoying the party.

Fleischer had only been in bed for a couple of hours when he was shaken awake by a terrified and trembling Tim Hayter, who told him that there had been a tragedy at the party. Hayter claimed that Helen and Johannes had fallen to their deaths from the balcony while having sex.

Dr Arnot told the court that he had only spent three hours at the party before leaving for a tour of the hospital to check on patients who had undergone surgery earlier that day. When he returned, around 2 a.m., tired and weary, he had gone to bed. He had slept soundly until his wife woke him around 5.30 a.m. to tell him, 'something terrible has happened. Helen and Johannes have fallen from the balcony.'

He had gone down to the forecourt and saw Helen's body crumpled at the foot of the building. But he didn't see any signs of violence on her body. Johannes Otten's body was a few feet away. He was not lying on the forecourt, but was slumped across a set of low pointed railings, his legs gruesomely impaled by the sharp spikes. His trousers were missing and he was wearing only a pair of underpants.

In the street, Arnot found Otten's passport and some private papers. Otten's trousers were never found. There was no sign of them inside the Arnots' flat, and the doctor said he presumed that some passing heartless thief had stolen the trousers from the corpse and thrown away the passport.

Dr Arnot admitted that his next concern, as a matter of urgency, was to get back inside his flat and try to hide all evidence of illicit alcohol.

Frenchman Jacques Texier was able to add more detail. He said he had seen Helen and Otten out on the balcony when he had gone into the kitchen to make himself a sandwich. When it was pointed out to him that the kitchen window looked out on to a different balcony, he changed his evidence, saying he had seen them from another window.

At about 3 a.m. he had asked Mrs Arnot if he could stay the night at the flat, because he did not want to wake up the official at the French Embassy who had offered him a bed for the night. Penelope Arnot agreed, and after the German guests had left Texier stretched out on a sofa. He did not notice where Helen Smith and Johannes Otten had gone, but he was wakened from his sleep around 5 a.m. by the unmistakeable sound of Mrs Arnot and Tim Hayter making passionate love in the room beside him. Later, all three of them had gone into the kitchen to make coffee. When they strolled unsuspectingly out on to the balcony, they were startled to see the two bodies beneath them.

The inquest also heard from witness Dr Hag Abdel Rachman, a gynaecologist who lived in the same block of flats. He had been wakened by the building's night porter and told there were two bodies outside the block. Dr Rachman said: 'I went to investigate and saw the man hanging upside down on an iron bar. The girl was on the ground, wearing a blue dress and no underwear, there was no blood or indications of violence.'

Dr Rachman gave one vital piece of evidence which left all the other witnesses puzzled. He testified he had knocked on Doctor Arnot's door after the discovery, and the surgeon opened it quickly, saying: 'If you mean that event down the building, I know about that, leave it to me and I will deal with it.' There was a lot of noise coming from the flat and, behind Dr Arnot, the gynaecologist saw a mystery man – a white, short man with a beard – who was never identified by any of the party guests.

The inquest jury retired for eight hours to consider the evidence. After their deliberations they still could not say that Helen's death was an accident, nor could they decide if she had been murdered. Eventually, they returned an open verdict.

Ron Smith remained convinced that all the medical evidence pointed to his daughter having been beaten unconscious, possibly resisting rape, and being placed under the balcony to make it look as if she had fallen to her death. There was evidence that her sternum, or chest bone, had been fractured, perhaps by violent chest massage in an attempt to revive her. Johannes Otten may have been thrown to his death on the railings to silence him.

Helen Smith took her camera to the party. She carried her camera everywhere and was constantly taking photographs. Yet, when the Saudi police recovered it from the death flat, they told Ron Smith there was no film in it. Helen, they said, had taken her camera to the party but hadn't bothered to load it. Another camera in the flat that fateful night belonged to Martin

Fleischer; but when he developed the film he found that all the frames were double-exposed.

No evidence remains of the mystery guest at the party, the white, short, bearded man.

A decade after her death, Helen Smith's body was still in the mortuary in Leeds. Her father's struggle to find out how his daughter died continues undiminished and relentless.

After the inquest, which still proclaimed his Helen's death a mystery, Ron Smith said: 'Honesty and justice will prevail. Everything will be resolved in God's good time.'

Oscar Mike

When Aer Lingus Flight 712 departed from Cork in Ireland for London's Heathrow Airport on Sunday 24 March 1968, it should have been a routine journey lasting little more than an hour and 20 minutes.

On board the Viscount turbo-prop airliner were four crew members and 57 passengers. At the controls was 35-year-old Captain Bernard O'Beirne, one of the airline's most senior pilots, with over 6,600 hours of flying to his credit. More than 1,600 of the hours listed in his pilot's log book had been spent flying Viscounts, considered to be one of the world's safest and most carefully engineered aircraft. O'Beirne's co-pilot, 22-year-old First Officer Paul Heffernan, had 900 hours flying experience on the same type of tried and tested four-engined airliner.

The weather was cloudless and Captain O'Beirne assured his passengers they should enjoy a pleasant, smooth flight. But, half an hour later, the Viscount, codenamed Echo India Alpha Oscar Mike, was a tangled mass of wreckage sinking under the waves in the Irish Sea, and Flight 712 entered the history books as one of the most baffling aviation mysteries ever.

Despite a detailed technical examination of the crumpled remains of the airliner, dredged from the bottom of the sea, and the painstaking analysis of the last frantic and garbled radio messages from Captain O'Beirne, no real answer has ever been found to the riddle of the disaster which left Oscar Mike spinning helplessly to its doom. There was no evidence of a structural or mechanical defect which could have led to the crash; there were no signs of a fire or explosion and no indication of metal fatigue; the weather in the area at the time was good; there were no other aircraft in the vicinity, and the possibility of a collision with a flock of birds was ruled out because Oscar Mike had been flying so high. The only spine-chilling theory, supported by the accounts of eye witnesses, is that Oscar Mike was blown from the sky by a glowing red, supersonic, unidentified flying object.

Within five minutes of take-off from Cork Airport in south-west Ireland, at 11.32 a.m. on a perfect spring morning, the Viscount was climbing up smoothly through the 7000 feet level. Local Air Traffic Controllers gave Captain O'Beirne clearance to continue his ascent to 17,000 feet and advised him of his course for Tuskar Rock, the craggy prominence with its flashing lighthouse off the Irish coast in the Saint George's Channel, separating Ireland from Wales. The cabin crew prepared to serve a light snack to the passengers, who included more than a score of enthusiastic Swedish anglers happily swapping tales of the salmon they had caught during their week-long expedition in the lakes and rivers of Killarney. The anglers were due to catch a connecting flight at London to take them on the last leg of their journey.

With the sight of Tuskar Rock slipping smoothly beneath him, the Captain steered Oscar Mike along the air corridor towards his next landfall, barely 50 miles away, at Strumble Head on the rocky Welsh coast. Twenty-five minutes into the flight, Oscar Mike's radio made a routine check call, reporting that the aircraft was expected to cross over the Welsh mainland within the next six minutes. Everything was going perfectly to schedule.

Two minutes later the master Air Traffic Control for Irish flights, at Shannon on the west coast, radioed the Viscount and instructed Captain O'Beirne to switch his frequency to London Air Traffic Control at Heathrow to be picked up and guided by his new controller.

Captain O'Beirne was calm and unruffled. He acknowledged the message by repeating, confidently, '131.2' – the frequency for the control tower operators who were awaiting his arrival in London just 50 minutes later.

Then disaster, unexpected and violent, shook Oscar Mike from its flight deck to its tailplane. The Shannon Air Traffic Controller no longer had responsibility for monitoring Flight 712 and he turned his attention to other flights inside Irish airspace. Meanwhile, at the radio and radar centre in London, the controllers were busy plotting the paths of dozens of flights heading for Heathrow that day.

The crew of one transatlantic flight were already reporting their position to the control room and Captain O'Beirne should have followed procedure by waiting for that conversation to end before he came on the air to announce his own presence entering the London air traffic zone. Instead, he broke into the other radio transmission. His message to London simply said: 'Echo India Alpha Oscar Mike, with you.' There was no sound of urgency or distress, but his call irritated the controllers because it partially blotted out the other aircraft already reporting their positions. They waited for Oscar Mike to repeat his check call when the airwaves were clear.

Only eight seconds later the next report came. This time it was frantic and desperate, distorted by a roaring and screaming noise in the background. Captain O'Beirne was gasping as he wrestled with the controls and yelled into his radio: 'Twelve thousand feet, descending, spinning rapidly.'

The controllers could hardly believe their ears. Two other listeners heard the heart-rending distress call from Oscar Mike: the pilot of the transatlantic flight, nearing the English coast, and the flight crew of Aer Lingus 362, Oscar Mike's sister aircraft. Both pilots acted independently, checking with London Traffic Control to make sure that the emergency message had been received clearly. The London controller made repeated attempts to contact the stricken aircraft. There was no reply.

But Oscar Mike was still airborne. Captain O'Beirne, struggling with the controls, had turned his aircraft away from the forbidding mountains around the Welsh coast and he was already retracing his flight path back across the Irish Sea. Perhaps he thought he had a slim chance of bringing the Viscount safely down on the smooth, sandy beaches near Rosslare, back on the Irish coast, just over the horizon.

The anxious listeners got no clue. There was only baffling and ominous radio silence from Oscar Mike.

With fear mounting, the pilot of the other Aer Lingus flight, bound from Dublin to Bristol, aborted his approach to his destination and sped north towards Strumble Head, Oscar Mike's last reported position, to begin an immediate search. Unbeknownst to him, however, the final moments of the fatal drama were being played out 30 miles to the west of him.

At 12.10 p.m., a deckhand on board the German cargo ship *Metric*, steaming southbound through St George's Channel, ten miles off Rosslare, thought he saw a large bird close by suddenly whirl from the sky and plunge into the sea. He thought no more about it. At the same time another witness, walking along the shore near Greenore Point, heard a roaring splash, and saw a column of water rising from the sea just off the Tuskar lighthouse.

The routine flight of Oscar Mike had ended in tragedy, less than an hour after it had begun.

Within a few minutes of the time Flight 712 had been due to land at Heathrow Airport with its crew and passengers, a major search and rescue operation had been mounted across the width of the Irish Sea, with aircraft, helicopters and high speed launches hunting for a clue to the disappearance of Oscar Mike. By nightfall, when the search was called off without success, the news of the disaster was broadcast. At home, watching television reports of the missing Viscount, the lunchtime beachcomber remembered the giant water splash he had seen off Tuskar Rock and phoned his local police station.

As a general appeal for all shipping to watch out for wreckage or survivors was broadcast on the marine shipping frequencies, the deckhand on the cargo ship *Metric* thought of the silver bird he had seen splashing into the sea. Could it have been an aircraft, its size distorted by distance? Thinking the worst, he radioed search headquarters.

The following day, using the approximate bearings supplied by the two witnesses, the search was resumed. Within a few hours floating wreckage had been sighted, having drifted less than six miles from Tuskar Rock. Over the course of the next few days, 14 bodies and more cabin wreckage was found. There were no survivors.

It took two more months for the bulk of the wreckage of Oscar Mike to be located, lying in 39 fathoms of water. The job of recovering the sunken aircraft and beginning an exhaustive examination of the mass of twisted metal began immediately. Accident investigators began to piece together a grim jigsaw puzzle of the remains of Oscar Mike in a deserted hangar at the headquarters of the Irish Air Force at Casement Aerodrome, Baldonnel.

Most of the twisted fuselage, wings and engines of the Viscourt were recovered, but the tail plane sections and elevators were missing. One small section of elevator spring tab, a small control needed to trim the aircraft in flight, was found six months after the crash, entangled in seaweed on the coast of Rosslare, seven miles from the scene of the crash. The small metal flap couldn't have floated. Had it fallen off from the wrecked tail section as Captain O'Beirne tried to make a landing on the beach?

In the meantime, other eye witnesses had come forward with evidence, turning the disaster from an unexplained accident into a mystery of deadly intrigue. During the late morning on the day of the Viscount crash, hundreds of devout Roman Catholics in the small seaside parishes around Rosslare had been going to and from the celebration of Mass in their local churches. The first Mass, which had begun at 10 a.m. had finished and now the church bells were calling the faithful to 11 o'clock Mass. The precise timings of the church services and the ringing of the chapel bells had etched the events into the memories of the witnesses with reliable accuracy.

In the official accident investigation report published two years after the crash, the identity of these witnesses is masked by code numbers which refer to their sworn affidavits of evidence. None of the witnesses had noticed the

23

uneventful flight of Oscar Mike as it passed overhead. But they all heard and saw strange sounds and sights in the sky a few minutes later.

Shortly after the Viscount flew over Tuskar Rock, bound for the Welsh coast, ten witnesses near the village of Broadway, three miles inland, heard loud cracking noises and rolling explosions in the air, like peals of thunder. Four witnesses saw a high-speed object in the air, its wings bright red and its tail glowing 'as if on fire' as it streaked out to sea towards Wales. Another witness saw it turn sharply in mid-air 'as if fired out of the clouds'. A witness ten miles away from Broadway, across the sweeping Ballyteige Bay, saw the same object 'enveloped in a small dark cloud which travelled along with the aeroplane, swirling'. This was followed by a bang, which died away 'like thunder'.

The evidence of the witnesses is all technically consistent with a supersonic flying machine, trailing clouds of turbulent air from its wings and leaving a wake of booming shock waves as it streaks through the sound barrier.

The investigators turned immediately to the possibility that Oscar Mike had been struck by an air-to-air missile or had collided with a military jet fighter, but checks with Britain's Royal Air Force, the only operator of supersonic aircraft over the Irish Sea, only deepened the mystery. No RAF jets were in the area at the time and none had been reported missing. The only missile firing range near the flight path of Oscar Mike, the Ministry of Defence rocket range at Aberporth in Wales, had been closed that Sunday.

Government officials in Dublin made approaches to the NATO military powers to check the flights of supersonic aircraft. The answer came back that no jets had been operational anywhere near Oscar Mike. They even asked the Soviet Navy if any of their aircraft carriers had been prowling undetected around the southern stretches of the Atlantic where it reaches into the Irish Sea. They drew a blank.

In the final dossier, which drew a veil of mystery over the fate of Oscar Mike, the Irish government's official accident investigator, R W O'Sullivan, confirmed: 'There is not enough evidence available on which to reach a conclusion of reasonable probability as to the initial cause of this accident.' But he did reveal that only one theory, even though 'improbable', covers all the bizarre unexplained elements in the accounts of the Viscount crash.

In his report, R W O'Sullivan admitted the possibility that: 'While Viscount EI-AOM was in normal cruising flight at 17,000 feet, and within six minutes of reaching Strumble Head, another aircraft, which could have been a manned or unmanned aeroplane or a missile, passed in close proximity, possibly even colliding with the tail of the Viscount, causing an upset before control was finally lost.'

Hitler and the Occult

When Adolf Hitler set out to conquer Europe and build an empire he predicted would last a thousand years, it seemed to military tacticians that he had put his faith in the strength of his armoured tank divisions and the swift striking power of the Luftwaffe bombers. At the massed rallies of his fanatical followers in the giant stadium in Nuremburg, the crazed dictator entranced hundreds of thousands of his countrymen into believing that he had built an invincible war machine. Even when the tide of war turned against the Nazis – when the Russians began to repulse the sweeping attack of the Germans and the Allies liberated Occupied Europe – Hitler was still convinced that, through some miraculous intervention, he would triumph in the end.

As the Third Reich crumbled around the Führer's ears, and he still insisted that a miracle would save Germany from total collapse and devastation, his own generals began to wonder about Hitler's state of mind. Had he launched the Second World War not through his confidence in military strength, but in the belief that he could achieve victory using black magic, by appealing to the occult and holy mysticism?

Hitler had begun his obsession with the occult when he was a teenager. He had been deeply, and perversely, moved by a performance of Wagner's opera, *Rienzi*, which tells the tale of the rise and fall of a Roman Tribune. The young Hitler saw the opera as a metaphor for the destiny of his own nation and plunged himself into the composer's romantic world of Germanic myth and fantasy. He began to study the occult and a few years later, in 1909, the young Austrian became a follower of the eccentric religious leader Dr Jorg Lanz von Leibenfels. This former monk had abandoned his Christian religion and had formed a new cult in a run-down castle on the banks of the Danube. Here, he preached magic, occultism and race mysticism.

Soon after this, Hitler became struck by the power of a particular religious legend, which was to become an obsession and may have even led to his suicide more than 30 years later.

In the summer of 1912, Viennese economist Dr Walter Stein, an expert in early Byzantine and Medieval art, purchased a second-hand copy of an edition of *Parsifal* from an occult bookseller in his home town. The book was a 13th-century romance about the Holy Grail, the cup from which Jesus drank wine during the last supper. Throughout the Middle Ages, legends

25

abounded about the whereabouts of the Holy Grail as well as another powerful religious relic – the Holy Lance. In the margins of the slim volume he had bought, Dr Stein found pencilled notes made by the previous owner. They were mostly rambling little comments on mythology, the occult and the power of racial superiority of those descended from the Crusaders and Teutonic knights. Intrigued, Dr Stein asked the bookseller to put him in contact with the previous owner … and soon came face to face with the young Adolf Hitler.

Hitler amazed and intrigued Stein with his knowledge of ancient myths; but he also puzzled him by his sinister belief in the magical powers of the Holy Lance. Hitler had seen the Lance in the Hofburg Museum in Vienna. According to the tales handed down since medieval times, this was the actual weapon used by a Roman soldier to pierce the side of Jesus as he lay dying on the Cross. The Roman had experienced an ecstatic vision in which he realized that he had thrust the weapon into the body of God himself. From that moment, the Lance gained magical powers.

There were at least two other sharpened iron blades in existence reputed to be the actual weapon used during the Crucifixion – one in the Vatican and one in a Paris museum. But Hitler was particularly fascinated with the Hapsburg Lance, which had been passed down to the Austrian royalty from a long line of conquerors and military leaders. The Holy Lance of Hapsburg could be traced back to Antioch, in the Middle East, where it was discovered by Crusaders besieged by Saracens in the city. German folk legend claimed that the Lance was carried by the Emperor Charlemagne through 47 victorious military campaigns, and that it had endowed him with powerful magic. In fact, it was said Charlemagne died immediately after letting the Lance slip from his grasp. Later it was wielded by the Saxon king Heinrich, who drove the Poles out of eastern Germany. It was then passed down to the 12th-century conqueror Frederick Barbarossa, who had triumphed over the forces of Italy and driven the Pope himself into exile.

Hitler told Stein how he had been overcome when he saw the Lance on display in the museum in Vienna. He explained: 'I slowly became aware of a mighty presence around it. I sensed a great destiny awaited me and I knew beyond contradiction that the blood in my veins would one day become the Folk Spirit of my people.'

But the Lance remained firmly in the security of the museum for the next 25 years, during which Hitler's belief in magic and mysticism was to become more and more deeply rooted.

It was more than a decade later when Hitler, then the aspiring leader of the Nazi movement, decreed that his whole terrible political philosophy should be symbolized by one fearful mystic design – the swastika. The sign of the 'crooked cross' had long been a good luck symbol in the Hindu religion, where it represented the life-giving rays of the sun, and in Viking mythology it had portrayed the Hammers of Thor, the god of thunder and war. It had been resurrected in late 19th-century Germany by Guido von List, a religious leader who led his followers in pagan rituals and the worship of old Nordic gods. Finally, it was adopted by Hitler, who wanted a bold, instantly recognizable symbol to rival that of the Communists' hammer and sickle.

By the early 1930s, Hitler had already bemused many of his top aides by his childlike belief in mysticism. His Armaments Minister, Albert Speer, recalled a bizarre incident in October 1933, when Hitler was laying the foundation stone of the Museum of German Art in Munich. As the Führer tapped the stone into place, the silver hammer he was using shattered into fragments. Hitler recoiled in horror and told Speer it was an omen that powerful evil was about to strike. Hitler spent three months in abject torment until, in January 1934, the architect of the Museum, Paul Ludwig Troost, suddenly died. Even though Troost had been a close friend, Hitler gloated: 'The curse is now lifted; it was Troost who was meant to die, not me.'

That same year, Hitler had appointed Heinrich Himmler as the deputy leader of the Nazi movement. He watched in satisfaction as Himmler began to persecute Jews and Christians alike. Himmler drew up plans to outlaw all religions except the new Nazism, banning festivals such as Christmas and Easter and replacing them with his own neo-pagan rituals. Only one thing troubled Hitler about his depraved and ambitious deputy: Himmler claimed to be the reincarnation of Heinrich, the founder of the Saxon royal dynasty, and a previous owner of the Holy Lance of the Hapsburgs.

One of the Führer's closest confidants, Hermann Rauschning, wrote of Hitler: 'He wakes up at night, screaming and in convulsions. He calls out for help and appears to be half paralysed. He is seized with panic that makes him tremble until the bed shakes. He utters confused and unintelligible sounds, gasping as if on the point of suffocation.'

But all Hitler's hidden fears and insecurity seemed to vanish on 14 March 1938, when, as Chancellor of all Germany, he addressed a rally in the Heldenplatz in Vienna and announced that he was about to absorb Austria into the Nazi empire. As he finished his speech, his soldiers quietly entered the museum behind him. All the regalia of the Hapsburg monarchy, including the precious Holy Lance, was seized and carried off to St Catherine's Church in Nuremberg, the spiritual home of the Nazi movement.

Flushed with victory, and reassured by his possession of the Holy Lance, Hitler plunged Europe into war the following year.

For the first four years it seemed as if Hitler and his forces were truly invincible. Even experienced Prussian generals, the aristocratic backbone of the German Army, became almost convinced that Hitler possessed super-human powers. He directed one successful campaign after another, relying on a mere hunch or intuition which he refused to share with anyone else. They watched in dismay as his deputy, Himmler, held councils of war from his headquarters – a rebuilt medieval fortress in Westphalia, where the vast banqueting hall was laid out with 13 thrones, for the Deputy Führer and his 12 closest 'apostles'. And they were even more bemused when Hitler himself set up the 'Occult Bureau' in Berlin, employing favoured astrologers and psychics to help him direct the war.

Soon, the military planning sessions with the Chiefs of Staff were being postponed and interrupted while the impatient generals waited for their Führer to consult fortune tellers before important battlefield decisions could be made. As the lightning advances of the German armies were halted, entrenched and forced back, Hitler insisted on having more and more detailed personal horoscopes drawn up for him before he could decide on the next course of action.

Navy chiefs were constantly overruled and had their orders counter-manded by one of Hitler's closest occult advisers, architect Ludwig Straniak. Straniak, an amateur occultist who redirected the Navy's battleships through-out the Atlantic, claimed that he could detect the presence of warships by 'dowsing' over maps and sensing the locations of ships by psychic vibrations. He had impressed the Führer once by dangling a pendulum over an admiralty chart and pinpointing the position of the pocket battleship *Prinz Eugen*, then on a secret mission. After that episode, the German admirals were not in a position to argue with him, and they were often forced to send futile fleets off to do battle in totally empty seas.

In London, Hitler's reliance on astrology and black magic was well known to Prime Minister Winston Churchill and his wartime Cabinet. They even established their own tongue-in-cheek department of astrology and occult to try to guess the psychic advice Hitler would be given, and to react accordingly. One of their advisers was Walter Stein, the occult and medieval art expert who had escaped from Nazi Germany. Stein still had vivid memories of his encounter with the young Hitler, and he was able to predict how the Führer would respond to the prophecies of his mystic advisers.

By the spring of 1945, it seemed as if no power on earth could save the doomed Third Reich. But even as the Allied forces advanced across the Rhine and through Germany and the Russian troops began pounding at Berlin itself, the Führer was still predicting some perverse, supernatural, miracle would turn the fortunes of war. In October 1944, when Nuremberg was pounded by heavy Allied bombing, far from evacuating the civilian population, he ordered it instead to be reinforced by 22,000 SS troops, 100

Panzer tanks and 22 regiments of artillery. Next, he gave orders that the Hapsburg regalia, including the Holy Lance, should be moved from St Catherine's Church to a specially constructed vault.

In April 1945 the liberating American Thunderbird Division reached the outskirts of Nuremberg and began battering at the defences. It took four days, but on 20 April – Hitler's 56th birthday – the Americans finally achieved their objective. When they began the interrogation of the prisoners, a wounded and embittered SS officer revealed to his captors how he had sacrificed thousands of his men, on the Führer's orders, to ensure that the Holy Lance was not captured.

The Americans immediately began a search to locate the holy relic. Ten days later, 'C' Company of the US Army's Third under the command of Lieutenant William Horn tore their way through the rubble and reached the twisted steel doors leading to the vault. Shoving aside the shattered brick-work, Lt Horn reached out and grabbed the Holy Lance. The foot-long blade was bound with gold wire which held a rusting nail – one of the nails which, the legend insisted, had been used to fasten Jesus to the cross.

That night as the Lieutenant returned to his command headquarters with the sacred relic, now the property of the US Government, Adolf Hitler put his pistol to his head and killed himself in fatal despair. It was 30 April, the end of the Hitler nightmare. It was also Walpurgis Night, the most celebrated event in the pagan calendar, the high feast of the Powers of Darkness.

Amelia Earhart

When aviation pioneer Amelia Earhart roared off into the skies on 1 June 1937, she may have carried a guilty secret with her. The darling girl of the air, who had become the first woman to fly solo across the Atlantic and the first pilot ever to fly solo from Hawaii to California, was determined to add one more flying record to her list of achievements.

Amelia was willing to risk her life to make the first flight around the world by the longest possible route – the closest course to the equator, a distance of

27,000 miles. She was confident that she had the flying skill to make the gruelling journey and that her twin-engined Lockheed Electra 10-E aircraft was mechanically tough and reliable enough to carry her through the worst of the weather the Earth's tropics would throw at her.

But determined and self-sufficient though she was, Amelia Earhart could not hope to smash the world record again on initiative and guts alone. She needed help from friends in high places to make her record attempt possible.

There were certainly many powerful and important people who saw that cooperation with Amelia Earhart could pay dividends to suit all parties. Earhart would have to enlist the aid of the best technical experts at the Lockheed aircraft builders and the vast resources of the United States Navy for her enterprise. Without them, the project was doomed to failure.

Normally, the American aircraft builders would have been only too willing to promote and sponsor any move by Earhart to get herself in the record books once more. Her exploits of daring marathon flights had captured the headlines and the country's imagination, and had helped to convince a hesitant public that travel by commercial airline was becoming a safe and commonplace event. They helped to sell hundreds of small airliners to more and more new operators each year.

But in 1937, the planemakers had different priorities. Their production lines were producing fewer civilian aircraft and were being increasingly heavily committed to turning out combat planes for the US Army Air Corps and the US Navy. Washington was nervously eyeing the expansion of Japanese military ambitions in the Pacific and they had themselves begun a growing programme of rearming and updating the squadrons of America's own flying forces.

During the First World War, Japan had occupied the Marshall, Caroline and Mariana Islands and had managed to retain these under a League of Nations mandate. In 1934, the Japanese began isolating the islands from their Pacific neighbours. Both America and Japan had agreed, at the Naval Treaty Conference in Washington in 1923, that military construction of the Pacific islands occupied by either side should be strictly banned. Now American strategists believed the Japanese were secretly preparing their captive islands as giant munitions dumps, communications bases and airfields for an attack on the US controlled Pacific islands – or even the American mainland – in defiance of all the guarantees they had given the League of Nations.

The Americans themselves had launched a defensive military build-up in the Pacific, aimed mainly at developing radio facilities to control a series of direction-finding stations strung out across the ocean to detect any large movements of aircraft. The War Department had entered into a secret partnership with Pan American Airways to build a series of direction-finding

Amelia Earhart – she vanished mysteriously in the Pacific.

bases on Midway and Wake Island, under the guise of providing navigation facilities for the airline's trans-oceanic flights across the Pacific.

The years of hidden preparation by the Japanese were to climax in 1941, with their surprise attack on Pearl Harbour. Even by 1937, the troubled skies over the Pacific were no place for amateur pilots to tax strained diplomatic relations by making trail-blazing publicity stunts in their aircraft. Amelia Earhart, however, was no unknown amateur. She had served as a lecturer and counsellor at the Purdue Research Foundation at Purdue University in Lafayette, Indiana; and the Foundation openly admitted its aims were to conduct aviation research 'with particular reference to National Defense'. The research unit was also in receipt of government grants backed by the US War Department, and the Foundation openly admitted it was providing the money to buy the Lockheed Electra for Earhart, for the scientific purpose of testing and improving radio direction-finding equipment.

In her eagerness to claim the glory for new achievements in flying history, Amelia had originally wanted to go one step further. She planned to fly the Pacific from east to west and carry out the first mid-air refuelling, using specially adapted US Navy planes. But the War Department ruled out her plan as too risky. Instead, they proposed an alternative, which would provide them with a strategic military bonus.

Amelia, they suggested, should be provided with a safe landing and refuelling stop in the middle of the vast ocean. The place they chose was remote Howland Island, only a few degrees north of the Equator and less than 600 miles from the Japanese-controlled Marshall Islands. Work began immediately on the construction of an airstrip and fuel dump, while suspicious Japanese warships patrolled around Howland on spying missions. Any muted protests from the Japanese were countered with outraged indignation on the part of the Americans, who explained that the airbase on the tiny speck of land, only three-quarters of a mile long and half a mile wide, was essential for the safety of the daring woman air pioneer.

In the meantime, Amelia continued with the preparations for her record-breaking flight and her aircraft was flown to Lockheed's private factory for special modifications. Amelia's technical supervisor, Paul Mantz, tried to monitor all the changes, but even he was unaware that Lockheed's chief specialist in its latest top-secret radio gear, Joseph Gurr, was detailed to fit experimental direction-finding equipment inside the plane.

On 17 March, Amelia set out on the first leg of the trip. But this proved only to be a disastrous false start after the first 2,410 miles, from San Francisco to Honolulu, had been covered. On take-off from Honolulu, overburdened with the weight of 1,100 US gallons of fuel and two navigators, the Electra crashed and its undercarriage collapsed.

Amelia sat down to an urgent conference with her technical advisors and her husband, George Palmer Putnam, and changed her plans completely. The flight would now circumnavigate the globe from west to east. With the help of prevailing winds on the new route, she would be able to dispense with the weight of one navigator and give herself some margin of safety. (The delay in her plans also gave the US Navy and the Army Air Corps a valuable breathing space in which to instal more and more secret defence equipment on Howland Island.)

On 1 June, Earhart started again from scratch. By this time her aircraft was bristling with a bewildering array of low and high frequency radio equipment and direction-finders.

There can be little doubt that, as she took off, Amelia may have realized that she had already become a pawn in the deadly mock war games the US military chiefs were planning in the Pacific. But for Amelia, her one goal was the successful achievement of her round-the-world trip. If her plane was being used as some kind of military flying test bed, it was a small price to pay for the chance to circle the globe. The flight was publicized every step of the way, with cheering crowds to greet her as she touched down, rested, refuelled and took off again from the various airfields in South America, Africa, Asia and Australia.

A month after her voyage had begun, her navigator, Captain Frederick Noonan, strapped himself into the cockpit behind her and the pair prepared for take-off from Lae, in New Guinea, for the riskiest part of the flight. Their course was to go over a stretch of the Pacific never crossed by an aircraft before – the 2,556 miles from the coast of New Guinea to Howland Island. It was the major leg of the flight across open water. The next stop should have been Honolulu, then Oakland in San Francisco Bay and finally home in triumph to Lafayette, Indiana.

The flight plan between Lae and Howland island was also the most crucial part of the journey for the US Navy's warship *Ontario* and the Coastguard cutter USS *Itasca*, supposedly acting as safety and rescue standby vessels, but secretly using Earhart's Electra as a 'target' plane to check and test their direction-finding equipment. As Amelia took off, the American radio operator in Lae, Harry Balfour, received a weather forecast on his radio and teleprinter from the US Navy Fleet base at Pearl Harbour. Although he called the information through to Earhart and her navigator several times, he received no reply.

Just five hours after his transmission, at 3 p.m., Balfour picked up Amelia's voice, clear and unflustered. All seemed to be going well. Two hours later the pilot radioed again, this time reporting that adverse weather conditions were forcing her to lose height and speed. But she was still unconcerned.

In mid-ocean, on board the warship *Ontario*, navigation officer Lieutenant Horace Blakeslee, who had estimated the plane should be overhead at 10 p.m., failed to make radio contact, although one of his deck officers thought he heard the sound of an aircraft overhead. The *Ontario*'s searchlights were switched on full, but heavy rain clouds had blotted out the sky. The warship, low on fuel supplies, was soon forced to return to base on a nearby island, and to leave the task of locating Amelia and her plane to the Coast Guard vessel *Itasca* almost 1,000 miles further along the course, off Howland Island. As the *Ontario* turned away, a land-based radio operator on Nauru island to the north picked up a broadcast from her, reporting the words: 'A ship in sight ahead.'

In the early hours of the morning, at 2.45 a.m., the radio room of the *Itasca* heard Amelia's voice on the radio again. The only part of the message they could understand was: 'Cloudy weather ... cloudy.' On the island itself, a top-secret high frequency radio direction-finder failed to track the location of the transmissions.

An hour later Amelia broadcast again, forlornly reporting overcast weather and asking the Coastguard ship to contact her on a new radio frequency. Again, they failed to locate her or raise her on the radio. Throughout the night they heard sporadic plaintive calls from Amelia Earhart, fragments of weary speech, but despite all their high-powered equipment they still could not reach her.

At 8.43 a.m. came Amelia's final message, frantic and desperate. She gave a confusing, wide-ranging compass position, which could have put her anywhere on a line stretching hundreds of miles both north or south of Howland Island. Then, all contact was lost for good, and soon the massive, but fruitless search began.

President Franklin Roosevelt personally ordered the battleship USS *Colorado* from Hawaii to steam full-speed to the search area with its three catapult-launched spotter aircraft. The following day he instructed the aircraft carrier USS *Lexington* and three destroyers to set off on a ten-day voyage from the west coast of America to join the search.

Nervous US Navy senior brass, who had secretly organized the seemingly innocent Earhart flight as an experimental trial, now began to complain they were 'spending millions of dollars and disrupting Navy training schedules to search for a couple of stunt fliers'.

There were a spate of heartless and cruel hoax calls from American radio hams, claiming that they had picked up distress messages from Amelia. Some claimed she was 'injured but alive' and quoted her call sign – KHAQQ.

On 5 July newspaper stories reported that a radio message had been picked up from Amelia by the Pan American Airways bases on Midway and Wake

Island. The message indicated that Amelia had been forced down several miles south-east of Howland, near the Phoenix Islands. War Department chiefs rushed to deny the reports, afraid that the Japanese might learn of the existence and power of these covert radio installations. For two weeks, an entire task force of US warships and planes scoured more than 150,000 square miles of the Pacific, skirting the Japanese-held islands to the north.

Then, speculation erupted among the more sceptical and scandal-hungry Americans that Amelia Earhart had been on a mission for the Government and had landed safely on Howland Island, in order to give the War Department an excuse to send warships and aircraft to spy on the Japanese war preparations in the Pacific. There were reports that US pilots, supposedly engaged in the search for their public heroine, had returned to base with aerial photographs of Japanese bases.

The rumours persisted for almost a year. One newspaper in Oakland, California, began a series of articles about Earhart's disappearance. Their first issue claimed that the woman pilot had been lost because the direction-finding equipment on Howland had been supplied with the wrong kind of batteries and had failed the moment it was switched on. But Washington soon put a stop to this, and no further articles were published.

Amelia Earhart and Captain Noonan were never seen again. Three years later, after the attack on Pearl Harbour and the overwhelming carnage of the war in the Pacific, the fate of the two fliers paled into insignificance until, as America fought back against the Japanese and began to drive them westward across the ocean, the mystery of Amelia Earhart slowly began to unravel.

Then it suddenly deepened again. In 1944, the victorious US forces captured the Marshall Islands from the Japanese. During routine interrogation, Vice Admiral Edgar Cruise was told by a native interpreter that two American fliers, a man and a woman, had been brought to the islands by Japanese captors in 1937. The couple had been transferred to the grim Garapon Prison at Japanese military headquarters in Saipan in the Mariana Islands. The woman was dispirited and broken. After only a few months in the hellish conditions of the military torture centre, she died of dysentery. Her male companion, of no further use to his interrogators, was executed.

Twenty years later, in 1964, two former US Marines, who had served in the Pacific, announced publicly that they had recovered the remains of Amelia Earhart and Frederick Noonan from unmarked graves on Saipan in July 1944 and had transferred them back to the United States for burial. But the US Marine Corps still refuses to confirm or deny their stories.

And so, the mystery remains. Was Amelia Earhart an intrepid espionage agent who gave her life to help her country develop its air defences? Did she die an unsung heroine with her brave navigator in the squalor of a

Japanese prison camp? Is she buried in a secret grave back in her American homeland with the location of her final resting place known only to a handful of military intelligence officials? Or was she simply an enthusiastic amateur glory-seeker who didn't care who organized and subsidized her daring exploits, just as long as she made the headlines?

The unemotional answer may lie in a report in a small Australian newspaper, published a year after her disappearance. The Sydney newspaper claimed that the United States had secretly informed the Australian Government, their Pacific ally, of their plans to monitor Amelia's last flight as cover for its preparations for war. The US War Department, which made great propaganda of the treachery of the Japanese sneak attack on Pearl Harbour, had refused to admit that it had duped her into a peacetime spying mission. The newspaper claimed the last distress signal had, in fact, come from the location of the Phoenix Islands, but the search squadrons used it as an excuse to turn north and spy on the potential enemy.

The paper concluded: 'Sentiment comes second to Secret Service.'

The Psychic Detectives

Even the most puzzling of murder mysteries usually yield, in the end, to patient, plodding detective work. The breakthrough can often come when the murderer makes a slip-up, giving himself or herself away, when a nosy neighbour makes an anonymous phone call to the local police station, or when villains argue among each other and turn to betrayal. Sometimes a mundane piece of police routine, a random check on parking tickets, or another tedious interview with a witness to check an insignificant detail can bring spectacular results. Even, in very rare cases, when every avenue has been explored and the secrets remain, a case can be cracked by a policeman's illogical hunch, or an investigator's unexplained instinct, which leads to the vital piece of evidence to unravel an apparently baffling, insoluble crime.

But when all else has failed, when the trail has gone cold and the case is marked 'UNSOLVED', is there one last hope? Is it possible for supernatural sleuths, psychic detectives, to see beyond the limited horizons of tangible evidence? Is it possible they can succeed in prising hidden clues from spiritual vibrations at the scene of a crime simply from the feel of inanimate objects, such as clothes or a cold weapon? Can people have 'visions', provoked by a lifeless photograph, or from the testimony of dead victims beyond the grave?

Most police forces scoff at the idea of accepting the help of psychic detectives, especially in serious cases such as murder. Often, they have to cope with cranks and deranged amateurs who plague them with tip-offs and bizarre theories. Usually there is no time for them to be taken seriously. Occasionally, after a case is cracked, the detectives allow themselves the satisfaction of revealing how so-called gifted psychics proved to be as worthless and as troublesome as any other time-wasting crackpots.

It is a brave psychic who risks his reputation publicly by making predictions in a murder case. Unlike seances and stage shows, where their apparently supernatural powers are often aided by collusion and harmless amateur psychology, meddling in an unsolved crime usually leads to charlatans being exposed. But often, police forces have to bow to pressure to lend a polite, if disbelieving, ear to psychics when distraught relatives plead with them to leave no stone unturned, when public opinion is crying out for some sign of progress or when a higher authority makes it known that a favoured clairvoyant should be consulted.

Such was the case in the investigations of the baffling Jack the Ripper murders in East London in 1888.

Robert James Lees was a celebrated spiritualist, whose psychic powers were reckoned to be so outstanding that Queen Victoria consulted him when he was only 13 years old. Other consultations and private royal seances followed, and Lees's reputation soared. So, when Lees approached the police investigating the Jack the Ripper murders, and explained the importance of his royal patronage, they could not show him the door of their Whitechapel police station as quickly as they might have wished. Queen Victoria had, herself, been bombarded with petitions from the fearful women residents of the East End of London as well as the worthy businessmen of the City area adjacent to the scenes of the horrific unsolved murders in Whitechapel. So, when James Lees claimed that he had suffered a harrowing psychic vision of one of the murders being committed, he was treated with some consideration and referred to senior officers.

Lees described the villain known as Jack the Ripper as a man wearing a dark tweed suit and a light coloured overcoat which he used to cover up his bloodstained shirt. Details of Lees's visions were duly noted. The clairvoyant admitted he was so shaken by the experience that he had gone abroad afterwards to France for a brief holiday to calm his nerves. A few weeks later, when he returned to London, he had another experience. As he boarded a horse-drawn omnibus at Shepherd's Bush in west London, he came face to face with the very man he had seen in his visions of the murders.

Lees had blurted out his fears to the other astonished passengers, including the suspect and the suspect's wife. The couple only laughed loudly at him as Lees fled from the omnibus and grabbed a passing policeman. The sceptical police officer returned to the top deck of the omnibus with Lees, where the laughter of the mystery suspect and his wife soon turned to indignation. While Lees and the policeman argued about whether to arrest the man on the unsupported word of the clairvoyant, the suspect and his wife slipped away, hailed a passing cab and galloped off into the London traffic.

Lees was devastated, but his tormented visions of the Ripper murders didn't end there. A short time later he arrived at Scotland Yard again, having had another vision, in which one of the Ripper's victims had her ears cut off. This time, Scotland Yard had to take him seriously. The police had received a gloating letter from the Ripper warning that he would slash the ears off his next victim. They had kept the contents of the letter secret. Even more important, they had just discovered the body of the Ripper's fourth victim, prostitute Catherine Eddowes, and the mutilations were exactly as Lees had described in his vision.

Lees then told them of a further vision he had had which seemed to match, in great detail. It was of the murder of Mary Kelly, whose disembowelled body had been found in a shabby lodging house in Miller's Court, right in the heart of Ripper territory.

It was at that point that Scotland Yard decided to carry out an experiment to test Lees's psychic abilities. That night, they took him close to the scene of the killing, a small alley which led to the door of the murdered woman's four-shillings-a-week lodgings. Their plan was to use Lees as a 'psychic bloodhound' to pick up the trail of the murderer. He set off through the side-streets and, in the early hours of the morning, the psychic led them to number 74 Brook Street, in Mayfair.

Seventy-four Brook Street was only a few miles away from the squalid slums of the East End, but a million miles away in terms of the social spectrum. The elegant mansion was the home of Sir William Gull, personal physician to Queen Victoria and her son the Prince of Wales. Gull had been created a Baronet by the grateful Queen 16 years earlier, when he had saved the life of the Prince of Wales by successfully treating him for a potentially fatal bout of typhoid. By now, Gull was a frail 70-year-old, partially paralysed from a stroke he had suffered a year before the murders began.

Lees pointed at the gates to the mansion and declared: 'There is your murderer – the man you are looking for.'

Even though their curiosity had been aroused by the clairvoyant's unshakeable assurance that he had tracked down Jack the Ripper, the police decided to wait until daylight before rousing Sir William from his untroubled slumber. The next morning, during a delicate and respectful interrogation, Sir William's wife admitted that her husband experienced occasional lapses of memory and had come home several times late at night with bloodstains on his clothes. Sir William explained these away as symptoms of the crippling effects of his stroke and the frequent nosebleeds he suffered. There were no further questions for the eminent doctor, and the Ripper murders ceased as abruptly as they had begun.

Mary Kelly was the last of the Ripper's victims. There were no more murders after the night that psychic James Lees turned up on the doorstep of Sir William Gull and named the Queen's doctor as Jack the Ripper. Sir William died 14 months later, after another stroke which left him completely crippled. And James Lees died in 1931, taking with him to his grave the secrets of his ghastly psychic visions of the Ripper.

However, in 1970, when medical historian Dr William Stowell examined Sir William Gull's private papers, the mystery surfaced once more. In an article in the journal *The Criminologist*, Dr Stowell claimed that Gull spent many lonely nights lurking in the darkened alleys of the East End. He also claimed that Sir William Gull may have been part of a conspiracy to cover up for another Ripper suspect, His Royal Highness Prince Albert Victor, Duke of Clarence and nephew of Queen Victoria. The Duke had been one of Sir William's patients and, according to Dr Stowell, may have committed at least one of the Ripper murders in a fit of syphilitic insanity, while Sir William Gull carried out others to raise a smokescreen and distract attention away from his royal patient.

Did James Lees really have visions of the royal doctor murdering the Whitechapel prostitutes? Or had he picked up more earthly clues from his own association with the royal family? Were his suspicions of Sir William based on psychic nightmares which revealed the truth to him, or did he point the finger at Sir William because he had listened in to gossip spread by members of the royal family, who suspected that one of their own inner circle may have been Jack the Ripper?

The mystery still remains.

There was certainly no gossip or insider information to help the psychic detectives who rushed to identify the beast responsible for the ghastly series of Yorkshire Ripper murders in the north of England between 1975 and 1980.

Doris Stokes (l) and the real 'Yorkshire Ripper', Peter Sutcliffe (r).

The murders made the headlines worldwide and sparked off one of the most baffling, frustrating and costly murder hunts in British police history.

The deaths of 13 women, most of them prostitutes but also a couple of respectable housewives and a young student, brought unsolicited help from psychics, astrologers and cranks who bombarded the hard-pressed police. Many of them claimed to have experienced detailed psychic visions revealing the identity of the Yorkshire Ripper, but the Yorkshire police tried to ignore their offers of information, putting their faith in the more tried and trusted police methods. They conducted thousands of interviews with witnesses and potential suspects, and launched a massive computer file, sifting through the few vague clues and countless hours of dedicated work by undercover detectives and beat policemen.

There were some apparently promising leads to the identity of the Ripper: a series of letters claiming to be from the murderer and a tape recording of the voice of a man with a strong north-eastern accent, mocking the police and boasting they would never bring him to justice for his crimes.

As a matter of routine, the tape recording was carefully examined by forensic scientists and voice analysis experts, and played to broadcasters at a press conference in the hope that someone would recognize the man's voice. No one knew, except, of course the perverted author of the tape, whether or not it was a cruel hoax. In fact, it was only much later that they discovered it had, indeed, been a false lead; but the tape was enough to spark off even more spurious information and tip-offs, which succeeded only in increasing the frustration and sense of hopelessness of the overworked detectives.

At the height of Ripper hysteria, in July 1979, the police were confronted by an astonishing story in a national Sunday newspaper. The article was illustrated by a vivid artist's impression of 'The Yorkshire Ripper', based on a psychic vision experienced by medium Doris Stokes. The fame of Mrs Stokes had spread throughout Britain as a result of her sell-out public seances. The newspaper report contained startlingly detailed information which she claimed had been psychically formed in her mind after she had listened to the tapes of the fake murderer. She claimed, confidently, that he was 5ft 8in tall, was called Johnnie or Ronnie, had a scar below his left eye and a balding patch which he tried to disguise by brushing his long, mousey hair over it. He was clean shaven, his surname began with the letter 'M' and he had received psychiatric treatment in a mental hospital. He lived in a street named Berwick, or Bewick.

This information, Mrs Stokes insisted, had been passed to her in a psychic trance when she had 'contacted' the Ripper's dead mother, a woman called Molly, or Polly.

The psychic floodgates were opened. Dutch psychic detective Gerard Croiset agreed with Mrs Stokes, and added the intriguing details that the Ripper walked with a limp because of a damaged right knee and lived in a block of service flats over a garage in Sunderland.

Clairvoyant Patrick Barnard disagreed with both of them. His own psychic vision was dramatically different, but equally specific. A week after the Ripper killed Leeds student Jacqueline Hill, in November 1980, Barnard revealed in the *Southend Evening Echo* how, in a psychic vision, he had looked down on the Yorkshire Ripper 'as if from my bedroom window'. He described the scene graphically:

'. . . On the shoulders of his black duffel coat were the white letters RN. It seemed as if he was walking out of a submarine dockyard. I felt I was in Scotland and I got the impression he was working on a nuclear submarine. Wouldn't that explain everything? A crewman on a sub, at sea for months at a time, while police are chasing their own tails looking for him ashore?'

Barnard also revealed that in his vision he saw an abandoned railway coach in a siding, where the Ripper changed his clothes after each murder before returning to his home – the top flat in a run-down grey house overlooking a railway tunnel.

Murder squad detectives suffered the spate of psychic clues and tips in stoic silence until, on 2 January 1981, the Yorkshire Ripper was arrested.

He was not mousey-haired with a scar and a balding patch; he was dark haired with a full beard. He was not called Johnnie or Ronnie. He didn't live in Berwick or Bewick Street, and he had never received psychiatric treatment. He wasn't a submariner; he didn't walk with a limp, he never frequented abandoned railway coaches, nor did he live in a house above a tunnel. His name was Peter – Peter Sutcliffe. He was a truck driver, who lived in a quiet suburban home in Bradford with his wife.

Sutcliffe had been captured as a result of plodding routine work. A police patrol keeping watch in the red-light district of Sheffield had spotted him sitting in a parked car with a known prostitute. A routine check, through the Police National Computer, had shown that the licence number plates of the car didn't match the registration details of the vehicle.

At the local police station to which he was taken, Peter Sutcliffe gave no hint he was a murderer. It was only while he was being routinely questioned about possible vehicle licensing offences that one of the traffic officers who had arrested him remembered that he had allowed Sutcliffe one brief favour: he had let him get out of his car and urinate out of sight in the shadows, behind a roadside fuel tank.

The officer had no psychic visions, no revelations in trances; no shadowy glimpses into the unknown; but he had a hunch, a policeman's mysterious sixth sense. He returned to the scene and found a blood-stained hammer in the shadows where Sutcliffe had relieved himself.

When the officer brought the evidence back to the police station, Peter Sutcliffe quietly began to unburden himself about his catalogue of horrific crimes, in a confession which went on until the early hours of the morning.

The Yorkshire Ripper was unmasked not by psychic detectives, but by the intuition of a suspicious policeman.

Chapter Two

MYSTERIES OF NATURE

In these days of high-technology, nature has still held back some of its most precious secrets. The animal world, for instance, is a constant source of wonder, with its tales of werewolves, flying fish and living fossils. In addition, we still have a long way to go to get to the bottom of *human* mysteries, such as miracle healing and the inexplicable relationships between identical twins . . .

Werewolves

Werewolves, half-man, half-wolf, have played a horrifying role in mythology and superstition. They are the spine-chilling, bloodthirsty villains of scores of horror movies, men turned into raging monsters, covered with coarse hair, with fangs for teeth, and slashing claws for fingernails. But are werewolves just a figment of the imagination, the products of the fevered delusions of poor peasants, the superstitious dwellers of the thickly wooded forests of medieval Europe and Asia? Or did they actually exist? And are there still men, and women, who can be transformed into snarling monsters who shun the light and attack with fang and claw to rip at human flesh?

Amazingly, scientific and medical evidence shows that werewolves may not be creatures of myth, but ordinary men and women – and even blue-blooded royalty – who have actually developed some of the characteristics and ferocity of wolves.

Tales of werewolves go deep back into history. Herodotus, the Greek historian in the fifth century BC, wrote of explorers returning from the settlements around the Black Sea with tales of local natives who could transform themselves, by magic, into wolves. Two centuries later the Roman administrator Pliny described how transformation into a wolf was punish-ment for anyone foolish enough to try to placate an angry god with a human sacrifice. According to Pliny, the victim would be taken to a distant river and forced to swim to the far shore. If he survived the freezing water, he reached the other shore only to be transformed into a werewolf, where he would roam the forests in the company of other packs of werewolves for a period of nine years. If the werewolf resisted the temptation to eat human flesh during that time, he would be changed back to his original form and allowed to rejoin his fellow humans.

Other myths and legends grew and grew. Men born on Christmas Eve were said to be more likely to become werewolves. It was also said that there were men who inherited the curse of the werewolf, passed on down through the generations from father to son as a punishment for some terrible sin committed in the past. Some men became a werewolf by choice, because they used the magic of the Devil to give them the power to change shape and to go about their evil deeds. And there were the benevolent werewolves, the poor unfortunates who could not help but change into beasts during the full moon, but who were bitterly ashamed of their involuntary weakness and who struggled to keep their guilty secret from friends and family.

The terror that the wolf struck into medieval man can easily be imagined. Packs of ferocious wolves roamed around the woodlands of most of the northern hemisphere and even the hot, dusty plains of India. Hunting in groups, they were a predatory menace to other wild animals, livestock herds, and man himself if they became bold.

By the end of the 16th century, wolves had been hunted to extinction in England, and within 200 years had been eliminated throughout the rest of the British Isles. But they were still prowling freely in the rest of Europe, where fear of the wolf showed itself in folklore, such as the cautionary tale of Little Red Riding Hood, the innocent girl lured to a grisly encounter in a woodland cottage by a cunning wolf.

During the 16th century, when the European colonies in North America were being settled, Henry VIII was on the English throne and Galileo was making his first astronomical studies with his newly invented telescope, France was in the midst of a religious frenzy where the mere accusation of being a werewolf resulted in thousands of innocent people being hanged or burned at the stake, along with other unfortunates charged with being witches and wizards. In one period of just over 100 years, between 1520 and 1630, there were 30,000 trials of werewolves in France. Most of those found guilty were quickly executed by their fearful fellow countrymen. Luckily, by the end of the 16th century, a growing sense of doubt about the strength of superstitious belief, as well as a feeling of communal guilt, led to more lenient treatment of 'werewolves'. After all, most of them were simply tormented and mentally deranged peasants, afflicted by lycanthropy, the belief that they could be transformed into werewolves.

An example of lycanthropy occurred in 1598 in Caude, northern France, when villagers stumbled across the half-gnawed body of a boy. They gave chase to two wolves that ran off as they approached. Searching a nearby wood, they discovered Jacques Rollet, a half-wild peasant who suffered from mental illness. He was almost naked, with a long hair and a straggling beard and claw-like nails which were clotted with blood and human remains.

The young boy had not been his first victim. At his trial, Rollet admitted to the judges that he believed himself to be a wolf and he confessed to several charges of killing and eating young children. He was sentenced to death, but the legal authorities in Paris commuted his sentence to life imprisonment and he was kept in a madhouse.

A few years later, the pathetic figure of 13-year-old Jean Grenier appeared in court in Bordeaux as a self-confessed werewolf. Jean was mentally retarded and his face was dominated by a large, misshapen jaw, which jutted out and

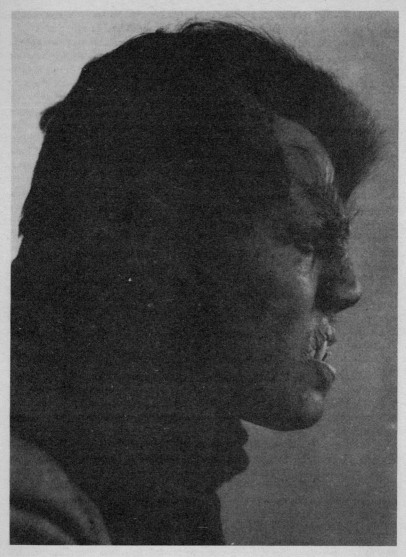

Half man, half wolf, werewolves are a horrifying sight.

revealed pointed, sharp teeth. He had been startled by some young shep-herdesses as he prowled among their flocks, and he had terrified them by telling how he had made a pact with the Devil to turn himself into a werewolf. When one of the girls was attacked a few days later by a creature with red hair and sharp claws, the townsfolk scoured the fields and forests until they tracked down Jean Grenier. In court the pathetic teenager stuck to his tale of a meeting with the Devil, in which he had sold his soul in exchange for a magic ointment and a shred of wolf's pelt which would turn him into a werewolf any time he wished.

There was no doubt that the boy was deranged, but equally little doubt that he had been responsible for several murderous attacks on children who had been killed and eaten. On 6 September 1603, Jean Grenier was found guilty of multiple murder while acting under the influence of lycanthropy. He was ordered to be held for the rest of his life in the Franciscan Friary of St Michael the Archangel. When the monks led their new prisoner to the Friary, he dropped on all fours and ravenously tore into scraps of raw, stale meat he found in their kitchens.

Jean Grenier lived only another seven years, howling at the full moon, unkempt and unwashed, still utterly convinced that the Devil had turned him into a werewolf.

With the near extinction of the wolf in Europe, the scourge of lycanthropy looked as if it might die out. Surprisingly, it surfaced again in modern times when Hollywood film makers hit on reviving the myth. In a new genre of horror movies, the werewolf and the human vampire were portrayed as 'up-to-date' demons.

In 1975, the myth of the werewolf so aroused one disturbed English teenager that he committed suicide. The 17-year-old apprentice carpenter from Eccleshall, Staffordshire, had become obsessed by studies of the occult, and had attended a number of seances in the hope of 'contacting' his dead father. At one of these morbid sessions, he revealed to a friend that he had become possessed by the Devil.

A few nights later, the teenager telephoned his friend again. By this time, the delusion of lycanthropy had taken an overwhelming hold of his imagin-ation. His friend later told an inquest: 'He told me his face and hands were changing colour and that he was turning into a werewolf. He would go quiet and then start growling.'

The young carpenter's body was found near the village crossroads by the postman next morning. He had thrust a knife into his own heart.

Although an attack of lycanthropy had plunged that particular teenager into fatal depression, it had a different effect on 43-year-old building worker Bill Ramsay of Southend, Essex. Ramsey went into a frenzied rampage in the local police station in July 1987, after he had driven himself there in a state of wild agitation. Inside the police station, he suffered a mental blackout, and fought a four-hour battle with eight terrified policemen. One officer was scratched across the face as Ramsey arched his fingers like claws. Others were hurled across the yard as they tried to restrain him. He was partly subdued when a doctor gave him a double dose of powerful sedative, but then he smashed his head through a one-and-a-half-inch-thick wooden hatch in the door of a detention room and had to be cut free by firemen.

Chief Superintendent Charles Harper described the scene: 'The man was snarling, his lips were turned back and he held his hands rigid like claws. He seemed possessed of extraordinary strength and attacked the men with a ferocity that was frightening to all who observed him.'

Ramsey was ordered by the local magistrates to be detained for 28 days for medical tests. At Runwell Hospital, near his home, he admitted: 'This has happened to me three times in six years. I do bare my teeth, I do drool at the mouth. I do snap and snarl and howl. I go on all fours, and my hands turn like claws. I display some tremendous strength and do incredible things, but I never seem to hurt myself. Why it happens, I don't know. I only know what people tell me happened afterwards. I just act like an animal. It's just a freak form of temporary insanity. The only thing that seems to affect me is walking into a church. I feel strange in churches. I can't explain it.'

There are a number of rational scientific explanations which appear to give some clues to the mystery of lycanthropy. According to medieval super-stition, a man who survived a wolf bite would later become a werewolf himself. The suspicion grew from the fact that the majority of those bitten by wolves would, within a few days, begin to suffer a horrific transformation. They would get fevered convulsions, their facial muscles would tighten into spasms which bared their teeth. Then they would fly into wild fevered fits and begin to foam at the mouth. This was usually followed by collapse, and then death.

These are symptoms known only too well to modern doctors as the clinical effects of rabies. Most wild wolf packs are infected with the virus, and those animals savage enough to attack men are also most likely to be suffering from the disease themselves.

However, not all recorded cases of men behaving like mad animals were caused by a bite from a rabid wolf. The potent medicines of the day included extracts from plants and animals, such as mushrooms or toads. These could often cause wild fantasies, including the delusions of turning into an animal. Even the grain storage methods caused the spread of the fungus ergot, which produces a natural version of the drug LSD, lysergic acid diethylamide. Many 'werewolves' were merely experiencing the wild horrors of 'bad acid trips'.

Some could also have been sufferers of the rare disease porphyria. The disease causes mental confusion, which can border on madness, excessive growth of hair, contraction of the muscles to reveal the teeth, and a necessity to hide in dark places, away from the sunlight which the sufferers find too painful. Sufferers also experience a need to take blood from others, to replace the constituents missing in their own system.

There is nothing demonic about porphyria. It is an inherited metabolic disease, once known as the 'Royal Disease', because its victims included Mary Queen of Scots, James I and George III. In King George III, the disease was so pronounced that his fits of madness and his bizarre, ranting behaviour almost brought the government of the country to a halt. His wild delusions about his own powers in stemming the disaffections among the British colonies in America, was said to have provoked the American War of Independence.

Although George III reigned for 60 years, for the last decade of his life, when his insanity became permanent and reduced him to behaving like a degenerate animal, his son, George, had to rule for him as Prince Regent from 1811 until his death in 1820.

It seems remarkable to think that America might still be British had it not been for a king who, by medieval definition, was a mad werewolf!

Miracle Healing

In these days of high technology, medical science discovers more and more wonder-drugs daily. These drugs seem to hold out the promise of curing the few remaining unconquered diseases and ailments in the world today. Each year, billions of pounds are spent on research to find yet more ways of keeping the human body fit and healthy. In such a climate of scientific progress, faith healers appear to be an anomaly. But as the numbers of drugs increase, so do the number of people who seem unaffected by their potency. Many incurable and dying patients put aside cynicism and turn to that last hope, the chance of a miracle cure.

It is not difficult for Christians to forsake the clinical methods of drugs and surgery, for Jesus himself was one of the best-documented faith healers of all time, with more than 40 miraculous cures, ranging from curing the lame and crippled to helping the mentally ill achieve full recovery. He cured lepers and made the blind see. All these incidents are recorded in graphic detail in the New Testament.

According to the Bible, Christ's Apostles were imbued with the same powers, and believers have no doubt that the power of prayer can sometimes effect a cure when conventional methods have proved useless.

Sometimes it is individuals who appear to have these strange gifts; but certain places have also become renowned for their mysterious healing properties and have become popular places of pilgrimage for those who are desperate for help. Springs, wells and rivers are often associated with miracle cures, like the Shrine of the Madonna of the Baths of Scafati in Italy, St Moritz in Switzerland and Grisy in France.

The most famous is the little town of Lourdes in south-west France, a favourite haven for the hopeful. In 1858 a 14-year-old peasant girl, Bernadette Soubirous, claimed to have had a series of visions of the Virgin Mary over a six-month period. The visions, she explained, revealed to her the existence of a hidden spring in an underground grotto which she was told had miraculous curative powers.

The visions were declared authentic by the Pope in 1862, and the cult of Our Lady of Lourdes has become one of the most fervent of the Roman Catholic Church. Now, more than three million people make the pilgrimage every year, seeking help. And for at least a few of them, the relief they seek so devoutly seems to be given. Crippled limbs are made strong again, diseases conquered, tumours vanish.

One well-documented cure dates from the 1970s. Three-year-old Frances Burnes from Glasgow, Scotland, was flown to the shrine by her mother, Deirdre, after surgeons diagnosed malignant cancer and gave her just weeks to live. Little Frances bathed in the waters. A few days later, when she returned to the hopsital in Glasgow where she was expected to die, she began to make an amazing recovery. Within three weeks, doctors could find no trace of the carcinoma which had racked her little body with pain. A month later Frances was back at playschool with the classmates who thought they would never see her again. Her specialist doctor at Yorkhill Hospital, a Protestant surgeon who held no religious faith in the powers of the Lourdes Shrine, admitted: 'There are cases of spontaneous remission, or cure, of malignant cancers, but we don't know why some patients suddenly recover against all the odds. We can accept that the powerfully-charged religious atmosphere around a place of pilgrimage can sometimes have an effect on the personality of a patient and give them a desire to fight their illness. This positive attitude, born of religious faith, can only help if it gives a seriously ill

The Grotto at Lourdes is lined with crutches and other offerings.

patient a renewed vigour and determination, a will to live. None of this can have been a factor in the case of little Frances. She is only a little child and couldn't have been swayed by religious fervour. The odds against her enjoying a spontaneous cure are thousands to one. These events are not entirely unknown. But the odds against this happening immediately after a visit to Lourdes are incalculable. We have no explanation. In medical terms we can only call it a miracle.'

Religious inspiration has been credited as the source of most dramatic cures which have baffled doctors using tried-and-tested clinical techniques. But other specialists in faith healing claim that, apart from physical injury, most disabilities and illnesses have their source deep inside the human mind.

Charismatic healer Phineas Parkhurst Quimby, from Maine, USA, founded his New Thought healing movement in the last century after claiming spectacular results from meditation and mesmerism and laying his hands on trusting patients. Quimby believed that all physical illnesses were basically symptoms of disorders of the mind, and his New Thought movement taught that effective cures would follow as soon as the patient learned to heal himself, or herself, by the power of positive thinking. There is little doubt that Quimby goaded and encouraged seriously ill patients into positive mental attitudes to conquer a wide range of illnesses.

One of his young students, Mary Baker Eddy, took his philosophy of psycho-medicine one step further, and in doing so relieved the patients of the need to rely on their own inner mental resources to give them strength to cure themselves. She fused the principles of New Thought with her own intensely religious beliefs and founded the Christian Science sect, which proclaimed that disease was an illusion created by man and that sufferers could be cured of their ailments simply by the power of prayer.

French healer Emil Coue, who was a qualified chemist, had carefully studied the apparent success of the practitioners of Mesmerism, who cured the sick by putting them in deep hypnotic trances and laying hands upon them, insisting that a form of 'animal magnetism' transferred a mysterious healing force between them and their patients. In Nancy, France, during the 1880s, Coue conducted his own unorthodox, and somewhat cynical, experiments. To carefully selected groups of patients, referred to him by qualified doctors with prescriptions for powerful medicines, Coue secretly dispensed ineffective doses of coloured water. He noticed, to his delight, that the patients who were treated with coloured water, especially those suffering from ulcers and nervous diseases, recovered more fully than those who followed the doctors' recommended course of drugs.

To Coue, the answer was obvious. His experimental patients were not being helped by animal magnetism or the power of prayer to God. All he had done was to stimulate their own imaginations into believing that they were taking medicines that would cure them. He called his new techniques 'auto-suggestion', and devoted the rest of his life to teaching the sick to cure themselves simply by imagining that their illness would vanish. His slogan, designed to reinforce the imagination of the patient, was simple and stunningly effective. Many thousands were cured by chanting Coue's incantation: 'Every day, in every way, I get better and better.'

In the 1930s, when conventional medicine was still firmly based on the belief that all disease and illness had an organic cause beyond the patient's control, two young British doctors hit upon an apparently rational, psychological answer to the phenomenon of Coue's cures by auto-suggestion. Doctors William Evans and Clifford Hoyle of the London Hospital were conducting carefully-documented clinical trials of different brands of new drugs for the painful heart muscle disorder, angina. To ensure that the effects of the new drugs were accurately proved without any irrational effects of auto-suggestion or positive thinking, they split their guinea pig patients into two groups. They told all the patients they were giving them the new drugs, but one group was given simple bicarbonate of soda without their knowledge. To the amazement of the two doctors, the group being treated with bicarbonate of soda showed the most dramatic improvement. It was exactly the same effect that Coue had witnessed on his early patients whose prescriptions had been made up with nothing more than coloured water.

The outcome of these unbiased tests was reluctantly accepted into the techniques of conventional medicine as the 'placebo' effect, literally meaning a treatment which does nothing clinically, but puts the patient in a happier frame of mind. Doctors now accept that many patients are susceptible to the placebo effect, but since harmless medicines do nothing to tackle the root cause of disease, it is dangerous to use it as a form of treatment.

But if belief, faith, or even a happier state of mind only lull a patient into a false sense of wellbeing, how can doctors explain the apparently astonishing cures recorded by healers who seem to be able to conquer advanced clinical symptoms in seriously ill patients?

Psychic Matthew Manning was just a teenager with no apparent appreciation of art when the artist Pablo Picasso died in April 1973. A few months after Picasso died, however, Manning found he could sit at an easel and produce vivid works of art in exactly Picasso's style, claiming that the dead artist's spirit was guiding his brush from beyond the grave. The following year he published his first book, with remarkable drawings faithfully executed in the style of other dead artists, including Aubrey Beardsley, Leonardo Da Vinci and Paul Klee. Manning insisted they were not his works, but the psychically transmitted drawings and paintings of the dead artists.

It was not until 1977 that Manning discovered he also had a mysterious gift for miraculous healing. When the young English psychic submitted to a series of rigorous tests at the Mind Science Foundation in San Antonio, Texas, he was found to be able to alter the electrical resistance of human skin and to accelerate the death of certain types of cancer cells simply by touch and concentrating his mind.

Manning's first attempt at healing a stricken patient was almost his last. He was asked to treat a woman dying of cancer. She was jaundiced and vomiting, and she couldn't eat. 'I just held her in my hands and tried to influence the cancer cells the way I had done in the laboratory tests,' he later explained. 'Nothing happened. I left, telling her I would come back to try again, but I felt a sense of complete failure. When I returned six hours later, she was out of bed. Her temperature was normal, her nausea was gone and she amazed the nurses by eating a meal.'

That night, however, the woman died. It was two years before Manning tried to heal anyone again. Later, though, he took it up once more, not only in private sessions in hospital wards and scientific laboratory experiments, but also by going on international 'healing tours'. During a public healing tour of West Germany in 1981, Manning encouraged doctors to examine his patients both before and after his psychic healing sessions. The doctors reported an immediate 95 per cent improvement in the patients treated by Manning. In Bremen, orthopaedic surgeon Dr Thomas Hansen verified that the psychic healer had taken only ten minutes to relieve the excruciating arthritic pain in one woman's shoulder, a feat which could not have been achieved by orthodox treatment. In Freiburg, Manning even invited the wife of independent consultant Dr Otto Ripprich to submit to his healing forces. Frau Ripprich had been unable to straighten her right arm for several months following crippling nerve and muscle damage sustained in an accident. After five minutes of treatment from Manning, she was able to straighten her arm, fully outstretched, to the amazement of her husband.

Not all miracle cures have been achieved by the mysterious forces of the mind or by the laying on of hands. 'Miracle' healer Jose Arigo had no medical knowledge, but his astonishing cures through his violently crude methods of surgery and his bizarre medicinal concoctions baffled the medical authorities of Brazil throughout the '50s and '60s. Arigo discovered his own awesome powers when he was summoned to the bedside of the dying wife of a friend, together with other members of the family who were preparing to mourn her impending death. Suddenly overcome, he seized a kitchen knife and plunged it into the woman's body. From the gaping wound he dragged out a tumour the size of a grapefruit. He dropped the knife and the tumour into the kitchen sink, horrified by what he had done. A doctor was quickly summoned and he confirmed that the bloody mass in the sink was indeed a uterine tumour. To everyone's amazement, the patient claimed she felt no pain from the impromptu 'operation' and there was no bleeding from the wound. She recovered fully, but Jose Arigo, still reeling in confusion, had no memory of the incident. Later, he told the woman's family that he had sensed he had been taken over by the spirit of a doctor he called Adolphus Fritz, who had died in 1918.

As word of the incident spread, hundreds of incurable patients began to gather at Arigo's house in the small town of Congonhas do Campo. Most of them happily submitted to the rough surgery of the healer, who often simply thrust them against a wall and cut away at their flesh with an unsterilized penknife which he later wiped on his shirt. For other patients, he would simply glance at them for a few seconds and then write a prescription for apparently conflicting doses of medicines, freely available from their local chemists. After following Arigo's instructions, the patients found themselves completely recovered.

As Arigo's fame spread, so did official curiosity about his methods, and he was sent to jail in 1956 for practising medicine without a licence. He served only a few months in prison until the President of Brazil, impressed by the petitions of Arigo's grateful patients, gave him a pardon.

In 1964 he was arrested and jailed again on the same charges, but was allowed out of prison awaiting the results of his legal appeal to a State Court. The Appeal Judge, Fillipe Immesi, decided he would be better able to judge the case if he paid an unannounced visit to Arigo's home to witness for himself a session of surgery. When he arrived, Arigo recognized him, and even asked him to assist in an operation he was about to perform on an elderly woman almost blinded by cataracts in both her eyes. The judge, who held the patient's head steady, reported later: 'I saw him pick up what looked like a pair of nail scissors. He wiped them on his shirt and used no disinfectant of any kind. Then I saw him cut straight into the cornea of the patient's eye. She never moved a muscle, although she was conscious all the time. The cataract was out in a matter of seconds. The district attorney and I were speechless, amazed. Then Arigo said some kind of prayer as he held a piece of cotton in his hand. A few drops of liquid suddenly appeared on the cotton and he wiped the woman's eye with it. She was completely cured.'

Arigo's case was reviewed by the Federal Supreme Court, and the charges against him were dropped.

Even when he was not practising mysterious surgery, where his rusty knives left no scars or bleeding, Arigo performed miraculous cures by prescribing dangerous doses of chemical mixtures. In the case of a woman patient brought to him, riddled with cancer and suffering the effects of a colostomy operation performed because a tumour blocked her colon, Arigo ordered her to take powerful overdoses of medicine which should have proved fatal. During the consultation, Arigo just nodded towards his patient without asking about her medical history, while her husband, a German-born Brazilian, spoke to Arigo in his native tongue. Arigo, apparently under the influence of 'Dr Fritz', replied in fluent German. Then, Dr Jose Hortencia de Madeiros, a specialist at the Sao Paulo State Institute of Cardiology, anxiously administered the massive doses of the drugs prescribed by Arigo. Within a week the woman had begun to recover, and on her third visit to the psychic surgeon Arigo insisted she was totally cured. He told her to have the painful and uncomfortable colostomy operation reversed. The surgeons who later opened her abdomen to restore her severed colon could find no trace of the cancer which had threatened her life.

When Jose Arigo died in a car crash in 1971, he took the secrets of his mysterious surgical miracles and the shadowy identity of 'Dr Fritz' with him to the grave. He had always insisted that he himself had no surgical skill or training. Indeed, on the one occasion when Arigo plucked up the courage to watch a film of himself carrying out surgery with a rusty fish-gutting knife, he turned white and fainted!

The Disappearance of the Dinosaurs

Powerful and ferocious, armour-plated and unassailable, the dinosaurs towered above the other creatures on the face of the earth. With scales and claws, fangs and toughened muscles, these gigantic reptiles had evolved over millions of years to become the undisputed masters of all prehistoric life forms.

With flesh-eating dinosaurs roaming freely in almost every region of the Earth's single, global land-mass, man could never have evolved or survived.

The span of the Dinosaur Age is almost beyond our comprehension. Consider, for a moment, that 225 million years ago the dinosaurs reigned supreme, flourishing for a further 160 million years, while our own ape-like ancestors only appeared on Earth as recently as two million years ago; and modern man has only been around for a brief 50,000 years.

Somehow, in one mysterious cataclysm, the dinosaurs died out. On the evolutionary time scale of the history of the Earth, they vanished overnight. The disaster, which wiped out the dinosaurs and three-quarters of every other species on Earth, tipped the evolutionary scale in favour of small rodent-like mammals that grew and developed into dwarf monkeys, apes and, eventually, the human race.

Only one remnant of the Dinosaur Age still slithers through living experience of life on Earth – the crocodile; and even the largest crocodile is a puny creature compared to the giant dinosaur reptiles, such as the 325-tonne *Brontosaursus*, which grazed on vegetation, or the flesh-eating *Tyrannosaurus rex*, the largest carnivore that has ever lived – 16 metres tall, 12 metres long and weighing 7 tonnes. With a great armour-plated head one-and-a-half metres long, and a gaping mouth filled with double rows of razor-sharp teeth, *Tyrannosaurus rex* ripped apart and fed on almost every other species of living creature, from the sub-tropical jungles of prehistoric England to the swampy marshlands which are now the prairies of North America.

The dinosaurs themselves evolved, like all life forms, from early sea creatures. Great upheavals in the Earth's crust led to climatic changes. The oceans began to recede and a great landmass began to break the surface of the waters. As the Earth became drier, some sea creatures made the transition to land by evolving lungs and primitive limbs, to enable them to spend some time foraging for food along the newly emerging shorelines. Some looked like giant tadpoles, with a third eye growing in the centre of their foreheads. This third eye is believed to have allowed them to see clearly in air, just as their other two eyes were adjusted to underwater vision. In time, the two eyes grew to develop perfect 'clear air' vision and the lungs took over from gills to allow the new land creatures to survive completely out of water. The third eye became useless – but it has not vanished entirely from the life forms which grew from these primitive amphibians. Even today, hidden inside the human brain is the pineal gland, the size of a pea, which is the hereditary remains of the third eye.

But long before man's ancestors appeared on the face of the Earth, the air-breathing reptiles had spawned the dinosaurs. During the Mesozoic Era, from 225 million years ago until 65 million years ago, the adaptable and versatile species of dinosaurs ranged from the flesh-eating *Compsognathus*, about the size of a chicken, to the gargantuan *Brontosaurus*.

The dinosaurs were refined by the forces of nature until it seemed nothing could replace them on the evolutionary scale. Then, suddenly, they disappeared – so completely that, until 200 years ago, men had no idea that such huge creatures had ever walked on the face of the planet.

The first partial remains of a dinosaur were found by a farmer in a field near Cuckfield, Sussex in 1822. The dinosaur's teeth seemed to resemble those of the present day iguana, so it was immediately dubbed *Iguanadon*. But, as more and more of the skeleton was uncovered and pieced together, early archaeological scientists realized that it was like no other creature.

The remains were soon matched up with other finds in the plains of North America, where the first enormous limbs of the *Brontosaurus* were being unearthed; and slowly, incredulous scientists, now called palaeontologists, began to piece together the colossal jigsaw puzzle of the dinosaurs. It wasn't long before they began to ponder the mystery of how these seemingly invulnerable creatures met their sudden end.

In the late 18th century, German quarrymen began to unearth fossils of giant marine molluscs, great spiral shellfish called ammonites which grew as much as 4 metres in diameter. The ammonites had died out at the same time as the dinosaurs; so had most types of primitive plant life.

Theories about the cause of the death of the dinosaurs abound. Some scientists say that a gradual change in the Earth's climate killed off the vegetation – the staple food of some dinosaurs – while the carnivorous dinosaurs became disorientated and sluggish, unable to protect their eggs from tiny, more adaptable predators. However, the dinosaurs had survived, adapted and flourished during other periods of climatic upheaval. Hence, it must have been some far more violent and sudden incident that caused them to perish entirely.

The first clues to a possible answer came in 1974, when Dr Louis Alvarez of the University of California carried out tests on a layer of clay gathered from a site in Italy. The clay, he quickly discovered, contained levels of the element iridium more than 30 times greater than he would have expected to find. Apart from a volcanic rift, the only event that could have spread so much of the earth's iridum into the atmosphere, Dr Alvarez decided, was the impact of a meteor ripping into the planet's crust.

Although tiny meteorites are constantly bombarding Earth, only about 200 have ever been big enough to penetrate the atmosphere. Some of these have left craters on the ground, which have survived to this day; but a meteor capable of powdering the Earth with an instant sprinkling of iridium strong enough to wipe out the dinosaurs, would have to have been at least six miles across, releasing the energy of a billion Hiroshima nuclear bombs, leaving a crater at least a mile deep and several miles wide.

Surely, such a massive dent in the crust of the planet could not remain hidden. Besides, if such a huge meteor had struck a landmass, it would not

Why did the dinosaurs suddenly die out?

only have released iridium, but billions of tons of powdered rock and dust which would have plunged the Earth into total darkness for many years, wiping out all life. Since some life forms did survive virtually undamaged and the process of evolution continued, the meteor theory could no longer stand undisputed.

It was Dr Alvarez's colleague, the astronomer Fred Whipple, who came up with the only plausible answer. What if a meteor, or possibly even an asteroid, had plunged into the sea instead of land? The effects would have been different, but equally catastrophic for the dinosaurs. In addition to the dust thrown into the air, a thick blanket of steam would have billowed round the globe in a cloud miles thick. The oceans would have boiled furiously at the point of impact, and a surge of warm water would have been sent up, encircling the planet. This black, choking envelope of smoky mist would have killed off enough plant life to starve the fish-eating dinosaurs of food. And, as the dust settled and the swirling steam remained, the humidity would have overwhelmed the land-living dinosaurs and wiped them out.

In the oceans, only the creatures of the coolest deep would survive. And on land, only small, furry mammals with highly-developed metabolic systems would be able to cope and remain relatively unscathed. The little rodents, the ancestors of man, would have also been able to feed on the eggs and the flesh of the enormous dinosaurs, who were rendered helpless and vulnerable to the elements.

A meteor or asteroid large enough to cause a gaping rupture in the fabric of life would still be expected to have left some sort of mark. For instance, it may have formed an island, embedded in the floor of the ocean and rising above its waters. Yet, there is no geological evidence of such an interplanetary 'bullet' lodged in the skin of the Earth. Hence, according to Dr Whipple, the meteor must have splashed down into the Pacific Ocean, burying itself in the moving plate of the Earth's crust, which would have carried it steadily eastwards over the millenia until it became crushed against the continent of North or South America. Then, like all the other debris of the floor of the Pacific, it would have been forced down underneath the continental ridge until it became swallowed into the molten core of the Earth itself, ready to spew out again in the form of molten lava, forming new land to give more life to the inhabitants of the planet it so nearly completely destroyed.

Identical Twins

For most parents, the birth of twins is a double blessing. Sharing the same life cycle in their early years, it's only natural that twins should become patterned to look and act like each other. What doting mother can resist the temptation to dress twin children in identical clothes, to feed them the same diets, to offer them the same toys and playthings, to make sure that they attend the same school, staying in the same classroom and undergoing the same experiences as they grow up inseparably together? Small wonder, then, that many twins are conditioned by their upbringing and their environment to lead very similar lives.

But what happens if twins are separated at birth, if they are brought up independently by different families, miles apart in surroundings which are totally dissimilar? Amazingly, even if twins grow up totally unaware of each other's existence, scientific research has shown that separated twins can lead uncannily parallel lives. Some studies even suggest that identical twins, two babies who are born of the same egg in the womb, may act like one individual person occupying two bodies at the same time.

The vast majority of human births are the result of a single egg released from the female ovaries and fertilized by a single male sperm. In one case in 80, two eggs are released at the same time, and each one is fertilized by a separate male sperm. The result is non-identical twin children. Although they share the same moment of conception and the same birthday, the children are no more alike than brothers and sisters born at different times to the same mother and father.

In even rarer cases, a single egg is fertilized and undergoes a remarkable transformation. Instead of doubling and redoubling in size to become a collection of cells that develop into a single baby, the solitary fertilized egg splits into two and grows into identical twins.

Twins may look uncannily alike, but nature ensures there are subtle differences to set them apart. Even twins who seem to be physical doubles of each other have different fingerprints – although their fingerprints are often a mirror image of each other, perfectly reproduced but reversed. However, sometimes a pair of twins seem so alike, they appear to have duplicate personalities. It is this that is one of nature's most baffling mysteries.

Twins Freda and Greta Chaplin were at the centre of a bizarre court case in York in 1980 when they appeared before magistrates accused of harassing their next-door neighbour, truck driver Ken Iveson. The 38-year-old twins had hounded Mr Iveson for 15 years, waiting outside the glass factory where he worked, shouting abuse at him and hitting him with their identical handbags. The distressed women could not explain their fixation over the long-suffering Mr Iveson. They did not seem to know why they continued to follow him and taunt him. Astonishingly, they answered the court's questions in perfect synchronization, speaking simultaneously, as one person. Whenever Freda prepared to talk, Greta would form exactly the same words, apparently at the same moment.

The court was told the extraordinary story of their life as identical twins who seemed to think and act almost as one being. As teenagers, they were so alike in the way they dressed and acted and moved in perfect harmony that local children called them 'witches' and threw stones at them in the street. Some adults spat on them, some crossed to the other side of the street to avoid having to face them.

Examined by psychiatrists, the Chaplin twins were given a pair of grey coats, identical except for varying sets of green and grey buttons. The twins cut the buttons off the coats and swopped them over until they each had the same set of mixed grey and green buttons. Supplied with two different pairs of gloves, they simply took a glove each and wore the resulting ill-matched pairs instead.

But when given two different bars of soap, the twins could not see any easy way out of the dilemma. Having spent a lifetime of eating identical food and wearing identical clothes, they both burst uncontrollably into tears when faced with the prospect of having to use different soap. Then, at the same instant, they both found a solution to the problem. They cut the soap bars in half and shared them.

Interviewing Greta and Freda, psychiatrists found themselves listening to an unbelievably outlandish 'stereo' conversation, with both of the women speaking in word-perfect unison. Greta and Freda explained simultaneously: 'We are so close that we are really one person. We know exactly what each other is thinking because we are just one brain.'

The lonely women, who still lived with their excessively overbearing and protective parents, seemed to have only one pleasure, a ritual obsession with cleanliness. They used 14 bars of soap and three large bottles of shampoo each week, bathing together, grooming each other and washing each other's hair.

The twins were discharged by the magistrates and left the court hand in hand to begin a new life together, as residents of a local hostel for the mentally disturbed, although there was no evidence that they were maladjusted.

The ability of the Chaplin twins to speak in unison is rare, but psychologists have studied cases of an even more unusual phenomenon – idioglossia –

Twins Hans and Gernard Fischer – 'mirror images of each other'.

where identical twins develop their own highly complex language which is totally incomprehensible to any outsider.

Twins Grace and Virginia Kennedy, born in Columbus, Georgia, in 1970 baffled their parents when they began to speak in an apparently alien language when they were only 17 months old. As the children grew older they used only two English words: 'Mommy' and 'Daddy'. Every other conversation was held only between themselves, without anyone else able to understand a word. They even gave themselves their own names. Grace called herself 'Poto' and Virginia named herself 'Cabenga'. They only responded to these names, and they refused to speak English, although they could obviously converse, share a joke and make themselves perfectly understood to each other in their own secret language.

At the age of seven the twins were moved to the speech therapy unit of the Children's Hospital in San Diego, California, where experts tape-recorded their conversations. There were few clues in the unidentifiable dialogue of 'Poto' and 'Cabenga'. Analysts thought they could detect jumbled phrases of

German and English. Perhaps, thought the analysts, this was learned unconsciously from their German-born mother, who was bilingual, and their grandmother, who only spoke in her native German tongue. But the complex grammar, using totally unrecognizable nouns, verbs and adjectives, defeated them.

After a year of speech training, the twins suddenly abandoned their secret language and lapsed into clear English. Excitedly, the speech therapists began to ask them to translate the phrases of their unique code. The girls looked at them blankly. From that day on they spoke only English and remained silent about the hidden meanings of their private language.

But if living and growing together leads twins to think and act as one, what can explain the amazing coincidences in the lives of twins who live apart?

In Piqua, Ohio, in 1939, twin brothers were born to an unmarried mother. They were adopted by different families and raised without knowing of each other's existence. Adoptive parents Jess and Lucille Lewis in Lima, Ohio, were told that the twin brother of their new son had died. The same story was told to the Springer family 80 miles away in Dayton in another part of the state. Six years later, when Mrs Lewis completed the long adoption procedure, she told court officials she had called her son James. 'You can't do that,' they warned. 'His twin brother is actually alive – and *he* is called James.'

It was nearly 40 years before James Lewis tracked down his missing twin brother James Springer and arranged a meeting. Both men were astonished that their lives had developed along inexplicably similar patterns. They had both grown up with adoptive brothers called Larry. Both had identical interests and weaknesses in the same school subjects, and they both owned dogs called 'Troy'. They had both married women called Linda, had both divorced them and both had subsequently remarried women called Betty.

Their first sons had each been named James Alan. They had taken their families each year to the same small Florida holiday resort, staying at hotels on the same beach. James Lewis and James Springer both worked as pump attendants in petrol stations, and they had worked as assistants for the same chain of hamburger restaurants.

Independently of each other, they had both volunteered to serve their communities in different parts of Ohio as part-time deputy sheriffs and, unknown to each other, they both immersed themselves in the hobbies of carpentry and technical drawing.

Medically and physically they had shared the same history. Each was 6ft tall and weighed 180 pounds. They had suffered tension headaches and migraines at the same times in their lives and had recovered from the symptoms at the same age. They had experienced identical heart problems and other ailments at the same periods in their lives.

The case of the 'Twin Jims' sparked off an intensive research programme headed by psychologist Thomas Bouchard at the University of Minnesota. Bouchard undertook a detailed comparison of more than 30 cases of identical twins separated at birth and raised independently.

Long-lost twins who had been reunited were flown to the American clinic to take part in the research. They included Mrs Jean Hamilton of Paisley, Scotland, who had been separated from her twin Mrs Irene Reid, raised 400 miles away in Market Harborough, Leicestershire. On examination, both women were found to suffer from mild vertigo and claustrophobia. They had led scout packs as youth workers and had identical careers with the same cosmetics company. They both had a strong aversion to water, so much so that on visits with their families to the seaside they had the same unusual habit of sitting on the beach with their backs to the water.

Bouchard also examined the cases of Mrs Bridget Harrison of Leicester and Mrs Dorothy Lowe of Blackburn. Identical twins, they had been separated since their birth in 1943. Both women had married within a year of each other. One had named her son Richard Andrew; the other had called her son Andrew Richard. Both women had studied piano to the same level of tuition, and had passed the same music exams. Both had kept diaries for just one year, in 1960, buying the same type of diary from the same printer, and they had faithfully made entries for exactly the same number of days before giving up and abandoning their daily notes.

But the most unaccountable case of separated twins who had led totally opposed lives was that of Oscar Stohy and Jack Yufe. They had grown up thousands of miles apart, but shared the same personality quirks and foibles. They fidgeted with rubber bands they absent-mindedly wound round their wrists. They liked to dip buttered toast into their coffee. They read magazines beginning with the back cover and finishing at the front. They had the same weird sense of humour, which included the practical joke of pretending to collapse in a fit of sneezing in crowded lifts to scare their fellow passengers into fits of hysteria.

At first it seemed as if the differences between the twins could not have been more pronounced. They were separated in Trinidad in the Caribbean in 1933 when their parents quarrelled and became estranged. Jack Yufe had stayed in Trinidad, raised by his father, a Jewish merchant. He had religiously studied the Jewish scriptures and regularly attended the synagogue, and became an enthusiastic King's Scout. He spoke only English. His twin brother Oscar had been taken to Germany by his mother when their parents had parted. Tutored in the propaganda-ridden schools of the Third Reich, he had become an ardent Nazi worshipper and a junior member of the Hitler Youth. He spoke only German. When the twins met for the first time since infancy, at the airport in Minnesota 46 years later, they were almost identically dressed, with wire-rimmed rectangular spectacles, blue shirts with epaulettes, and sporting short clipped moustaches.

Unable to understand each other's language, the Jew and the Nazi embraced each other silently with tears in their eyes, two halves of nature in a most astonishing double act; identical twins reunited and made into one complete person again.

Fishfalls

For timber worker John Lewis the sudden shower of rain on 9 February 1859, at the sawmill at Mountain Ash, Glamorgan, Wales, meant that he had to pack away his tools and take shelter until the weather cleared. As he ran through the puddles of rainwater to reach the cover of the tool shed, he felt himself being pelted by a stream of objects falling from the clouds. Then, as he pulled the brim of his hat tighter over his head for protection, he found himself standing in the middle of a downpour of live, wriggling fish.

The brim of his hat was filled with fish, there were fish littered over the roof of the tool shed, and still more fish gasping in the pools of water at the amazed man's feet.

As the sky cleared, the astonished timber worker and his workmates began to gather the fish in some wooden baskets they had with them. Ten minutes later, there was another rain squall, and another shower of live fish. It wasn't a widespread spray from the overcast sky, but one solid line of fish, a 12-inch-wide stream of tiddlers emerging from one section of the clouds.

In local Welsh newspaper reports, Lewis described the bizarre shower of fish from the sky. He told how he felt the first of the falling objects glance off his head and slither down his neck. 'On putting my hand down my neck,' he said, 'I was surprised to find they were small fish. By this time I saw that the whole ground was covered with them. I took off my hat, the brim of which was full of them. They were jumping all about. The shed was covered with them. My mates and I might have gathered bucketfuls of them, scraping with our hands. There were two showers. It wasn't blowing very hard but it was uncommon wet. The fish came down in a body.'

To the Welsh workers the fall of fish from the sky was an isolated, mysterious wonder. However, great storms of live, and dead, fish from the sky are a worldwide phenomenon, which has been happening for thousands of years. Moreover, fish have not fallen from storm clouds whipped up by typhoons and whirlwinds; they have fallen from cloudless, sunny skies. In some falls, the fish have been 'quick-frozen' in blocks of ice; in others they have been dried and preserved.

Some of the earliest incidents are recorded by Greek historian Athenaeus in texts he gathered in the 2nd century AD from hundreds of writers living in the Greek islands. Athenaeus reported that his fellow writer Phoenias, '... in his second book, says that in the Chersonesus area it once rained fish uninterruptedly for three days, and Phylarchus in his fourth book says that the people had often seen it raining fish'.

There are also scores of reports of fishfalls from far more recent times. In February 1861, the island of Singapore was shaken by a violent earthquake, followed by six days of torrential rain. French naturalist François de Castlenau, who was on a research tour of the island, told the Academy of Sciences in Paris: 'The sun lifted, and from my window I saw a large number of Malays and Chinese filling baskets with fishes, which they picked up in the pools of water which covered the ground. On being asked where the fishes came from, they answered that they had fallen from the sky. Three days afterwards, when the pools had dried up, we found many dead fishes.'

American marine biologist Alan Bajikov witnessed a fall of fish in October 1947 while having breakfast with his wife in a café in Marksville, Louisiana. Sunfish, minnows and black bass came pelting from the sky shortly after a gentle shower of rain. Bajikov reported that although there had been rain showers, there were no whirlwinds or waterspouts (which could have swept up the fish from the nearest large stretch of water, the Gulf of Mexico, more than 80 miles away).

On two occasions in the 1830s, at Futtepoor and at Allahabad, in India, the fish that fell from the sky were not just dead, but neatly dried and preserved. In Essen, Germany, in 1896 when freshwater carp fell from the sky, they were encased in blocks of ice, as if they had been carried aloft in freezing clouds long enough to form into giant, scaly hailstones. And when a torrent of sand eels fell into the gardens of homes in Hendon, Sunderland, in 1918, the cascade lasted a full ten minutes, and landed only in one small, confined area.

There is no doubt that whirlwinds and tornadoes can scoop up light objects and small animals from the surface of the earth during a storm, scattering them over a wide area. However, in all the reported cases of fishfalls, fish have fallen from almost cloudless skies, unaccompanied by any other debris one would normally expect to be scooped up in a whirlwind. No one knows what the mysterious force is that can suck up fish from the depths of the oceans and lakes, directing them in one narrow funnel across a great arc, so high in the sky that they fall to earth over periods of days, long after any storms have passed.

Living Fossils

The engineers carving the great railway tunnel through the mountains between Saint Dizier and Nancy in north-eastern France in 1856 were experts with explosives. Confronted with a massive boulder of Jurassic limestone blocking their path, they set their charges, primed the detonators and retired to a safe distance to blast it in two. It took a few minutes for the dust to settle. Then, the labour squad moved back down the tunnel with their picks and shovels.

The boulder had been split neatly. But when they prised apart the stone with their picks to load it on to a rail truck to be dumped at the edge of the cutting, the workmen reeled back in horror. From the crack in the boulder, a hideous black bird was emerging. The bird was about the size of a goose, but it had a long savage beak lined with razor sharp teeth. Its four long legs ended in sharp talons, and spread between them was a thick leathery skin, glistening with a thick oil.

Slowly, the bird rattled and stretched its wings, its beak chattering as it choked desperately in the dusty air. It made a feeble attempt to flutter free down the tunnel, but only flapped for a few feet before it gasped and died.

The mystified workmen took the body of the dead bird to the nearby town of Gray, to a natural history museum, where an astounded expert immediately recognized it as a prehistoric pterodactyl.

The rock strata from which the living fossil had been freed is named after the Jura Mountains of the border of France and Switzerland. These are great soaring outcrops of limestone formed about 150 million years ago, in the

PREMIO   £100   REWARD
RECOMPENSE

Examine este peixe com cuidado. Talvez lhe dê sorte. Repare nos dois rabos que possui e nas suas estranhas barbatanas. O único exemplar que a ciência encontrou tinha, de comprimento, 160 centímetros. Mas já houve quem visse outros. Se tiver a sorte de apanhar ou encontrar algum NÃO O CORTE NEM O LIMPE DE QUALQUER MODO — conduza-o imediatamente, inteiro, a um frigorífico ou peça a pessoa competente que dele se ocupe. Solicite, ao mesmo tempo, a essa pessoa, que avise imediatamente, por meio de telgrama, o professor J. L. B. Smith, da Rhodes University, Grahamstown, União Sul-Africana.

Os dois primeiros especimes serão pagos à razão de 10.000$, cada, sendo o pagamento garantido pela Rhodes University e pelo South African Council for Scientific and Industrial Research. Se conseguir obter mais de dois, conserve-os todos, visto terem grande valor, para fins científicos, e as suas canseiras serão bem recompensadas.

COELACANTH

Look carefully at this fish. It may bring you good fortune. Note the peculiar double tail, and the fins. The only one ever saved for science was 5 ft (160 cm.) long. Others have been seen. If you have the good fortune to catch or find one DO NOT CUT OR CLEAN IT ANY WAY but get it whole at once to a cold storage or to some responsible official who can care for it, and ask him to notify Professor J. L. B. Smith of Rhodes University Grahamstown, Union of S. A., immediately by telegraph. For the first 2 apecimens £100 (10.000 Esc.) cach will be paid, guaranteed by Rhodes University and by the South African Council for Scientific and Industrial Research. If you get more than 2, save them all, as every one is valuable for scientific purposes and you will be well paid.

Veuillez remarquer avec attention ce poisson. Il pourra vous apporter bonne chance, peut être. Regardez les deux queuex qu'il possède et ses étranges nageoires. Le seul exemplaire que la science a trouvé avait, de longueur, 160 centimètres. Cependant d'autres ont trouvés quelques exemplaires en plus.

Si jamais vous avez la chance d'en trouver un NE LE DÉCOUPEZ PAS NI NE LE NETTOYEZ D'AUCUNE FAÇON, conduisez-le immediatement, tout entier, a un frigorifique ou glacière en demandat a une personne competente de s'en occuper. Simultanement veuillez prier a cette personne de faire part telegraphiquement à Mr. le Professeus J. L. B. Smith, de la Rhodes University, Grahamstown, Union Sud-Africaine.

Le deux premiers exemplaires seront payés à la raison de £100 chaque dont le payment est garanti par la Rhodes University et par la South African Council for Scientific and Industrial Research.

Si, jamais il vous est possible d'en obtenir plus de deux, nous vous serions très grés de les conserver vu qu'ils sont d'une très grande valeur pour fins scientifiques, et, neanmoins les fatigues pour obtantion seront bien recompensées.

Rewards were often offered for the finding of living fossils.

middle of the Mesozoic Era, early in the history of the Earth when dinosaurs roamed the planet and the reptilian pterodactyls, some with 50-foot wingspans, soared over the oceans and primeval swamps.

According to reports in the *Illustrated London News*, the pterodactyl had been encased so snugly in the boulder that the limestone was left with a perfectly moulded imprint of its body, evidence that it may have become sucked into a thick muddy swamp which, in the course of millions of years, had solidified into rock.

But how had the air-breathing reptile survived for so long, encrusted inside the swamp mud without oxygen or food, under the enormous pressures which eventually turned the thick soil to rock?

The case of the French pterodactyl was the most spectacular find in a long catalogue of discoveries of living fossils and reptiles in states of suspended animation uncovered by quarrymen and stonemasons throughout the ages. *The Annual Register*, a scientific journal published in Paris, devoted most of its pages in 1761 to accounts of petrified creatures which had shown signs of life when freed from rocky chambers that had held their bodies long after their species had become extinct. The *Register* reported, quite casually, that the limestone blocks used as paving stones for the harbour at Toulon, on France's Mediterranean coast, were often split open by workmen who found they contained living shellfish with a wonderfully delicate flavour and taste. It also chronicled the notes of Ambroise Pare, who was principal surgeon to the 16th-century King Henry III of France. Pare had described how he was supervising workmen breaking up large stones in the garden of his home in Meudon, outside Paris when: 'in the middle of one we found a huge toad, full of life and without any visible aperture by which it could get there . . .'

A similar tale was told by the respected scientist Dr E D Clarke of Caius College, Cambridge, who described his own experience of an archeological expedition to locate fossils in an English chalk pit. At a depth of 45 fathoms (270 feet), Dr Clarke and his team had uncovered a layer of long-dead, fossilized sea urchins and the bodies of three tiny newts. Since the newts appeared to be perfectly preserved in the moist chalk, Dr Clarke carefully spread out their bodies in a sheet of paper to dry in the sunlight.

To his amazement, after a few minutes, they began to move. Two of them died a short time later, but the third 'skipped and twisted about as well as if it had never been torpid'. Curious to see how the newt reacted to water, Dr Clarke lowered it gently into a pond, where it slithered out of his grasp so quickly that it was never recovered.

He later gathered examples of all the species of newts in local ponds, in the hope of matching them with the scaly bodies of the two dead newts he still had as specimens; but all the amphibians appeared to be totally different to his living fossils. Amateur biologist the Reverend Richard Cobbold of Cambridge, who attended Dr Clarke's lectures and examined the fossil newts for himself, proudly confirmed: 'They are of an entirely extinct species, never before known.'

Before long, Victorian England was intrigued by reports of toads and frogs being discovered, locked deep inside rocks and boulders. In October 1862, local newspapers in Lincolnshire reported a live toad found encased in bedrock seven feet underground during the excavation of a cellar in a tavern in Spittlegate, Stamford. Three years later the *Leeds Mercury* ran a long, detailed account of a live toad found in a 200-million-year-old block of magnesium limestone 25 feet underground, unearthed by foreman James Yeal during the construction of the Hartlepool Waterworks. The toad, whose skin was the same yellow-white brilliance as the rock, had some difficulty breathing when its prehistoric tomb was cracked open, but it soon changed colour to a natural olive brown. Unfortunately, even though it appeared to have survived the millions of years underground, it 'croaked' after only two days in the modern world!

At the same time as wild claims were being made about living fossil toads being uncovered, experimenters were trying to recreate the conditions themselves. In 1825, Dr Frank Buckland, the Dean of Westminster, had tried burying a dozen luckless toads in his own home-made fossil tombs. Buckland carved small cavities in two blocks of sandstone and limestone and sealed the toads under glass before burying them three feet down in his garden. A year later, he exhumed his stone blocks. The toads buried in sandstone were all dead. However, those trapped under a sheet of glass in limestone chambers were not only alive, at least two of them had grown plump and fat.

However, it turned out that Buckland's experimental methods had been faulty. The glass covers had cracked, and it was possible that small insects had crawled into the chamber and provided nourishment for the fatted toads. In fact, when Buckland repeated the experiment and sealed the toads securely, they all died.

Buckland's failure only served to spark off more ghoulish attempts to bury toads alive to see if they could survive. According to *The Times* of 23 September 1862, one French experimenter who had encased 20 toads in suffocating moulds of plaster of Paris and buried them deep underground, was rewarded by finding four of them alive and healthy when he dug them up some 12 years later.

Even though toads and frogs can quite naturally spend six months alive buried in deep mud as part of their normal winter hibernation, the rash of cruel tests eventually proved too much for Victorian moralists. The attempts to recreate living fossils were abandoned after Dr Buckland's son wrote a stern letter to *The Times*, lambasting the directors of the Great Exhibition of 1851 who were intending to display yet another example, a toad allegedly found alive inside a lump of coal in a Welsh mine.

The whole of this era is commemorated in the legacy of the meal of greasy sausage meat hermetically sealed in a skin of thick, suffocating batter, which the Victorian children immediately dubbed 'toad in the hole'.

The records of the French pterodactyl fossil still leave the intriguing question: what if there is a giant rock somewhere out there, containing a prehistoric reptile or a dinosaur in a state of suspended animation? And what if that rock is already lying in the path of a 20th-century construction project, where the blasting crews and the bulldozers are preparing to move in?

Chapter Three

MYTH OR FACT?

While many of us shrug off the possibilities of voodoo witchery, the 'living dead' or the baying banshee, there are countless people who live in mortal fear of them. And while we may scoff at the likelihood of there being fairies at the bottom of our gardens, millions of ordinary, perfectly sane people rush to the horoscope page of their daily newspaper to see what life holds in store. Then there are the mysterious legends, such as the puzzle of the buried corpses at Glastonbury Abbey. Fact, or fiction? Sometimes it's not so easy to tell ...

The Stars

When Ronald Reagan and Mikhail Gorbachev met at the summit conference at 1.30 p.m. on 8 December 1987 to sign the historic treaty eliminating intermediate range nuclear missiles, both world leaders were supported by their top military tacticians acting as their consultants. However, behind the scenes, the Soviet Chairman and the American President both had the hidden backing of their most secret advisors – the analysts of the Soviet secret service, the KGB, and a Californian astrologer! Remarkably, during Reagan's eight-year term in the White House, where much of his schedule and most of his top level meetings were organized by his wife Nancy, Ronald Reagan's presidency was firmly controlled by astrological predictions.

The belief that the power of astrology could shape policy and direct the President's life – and the destiny of the most powerful nation on earth – caused a storm of protest when it was revealed by his former White House Chief of Staff Donald Regan in May 1988. Embarrassed White House officials rushed to claim that Nancy Reagan's faith in the forecasts of the stars were never relied on actually to guide the President in any major political decisions. But their denials were brushed aside by earlier evidence of the President's own admissions that he and his wife consulted their horoscopes every day for advice on how to run their lives.

The Reagans are not alone in believing that the alignments of the Sun, the Moon and the planets in the sky determine not only the fate of everyone on the planet, but the destinies of cities, nations and the day-to-day running of business enterprises. In the United States there are 5,000 full-time professional astrologers, earning between them around $35 million each year from believers who are anxious to learn what fate has in store for them. In the US, Europe and throughout most of the world, more than nine out of ten popular newspapers carry daily horoscope columns, which are often the most avidly read feature for countless millions of readers.

Astrologers are consulted by business tycoons in control of vast industrial empires, by royals, by heads of government, by architects who want to ensure good fortune for building projects, by sportsmen and women who want to enhance their chances of success in sporting competitions, by famous celebrities in the world of entertainment who want to boost their careers, and by ordinary men and women who want to ensure a happy marriage.

American astrologer Joan Quigley, 'advisor' to the Reagans.

Which one of us does not know the name of the astrological sign we were born under? Which of us has not been cheered and encouraged, or depressed and dejected by reading a horoscope during a period of personal crisis? So why do powerful and important people squirm in discomfort if it is revealed they pay secret lip service to the most enduring, mysterious myth in the history of the human race? Can the movements of the Sun and planets in the heavens control events on Earth? If so, how do they do it, and how can we accurately interpret the signs in the heavens?

Astrology is the belief that the movements of the planets can affect us in our daily lives. It is not to be confused with astronomy, which is objective, scientific study of the heavens. Despite the fact that astrology has been debunked time and time again by scientists, and especially astronomers, its influence has been more widespread and has persisted longer than any other creed, religion or supernatural belief.

The history of astrology can be traced back to ancient Babylonia, now the site of modern Iraq, in 600 BC, when court astrologers began to draw up their first detailed maps of the movements of the planets and to relate their positions to periods of floods and disasters on earth. The first detailed handbook on astrology came from the Greek astronomer Ptolemy, in the 2nd century AD, when constellations of fixed stars were grouped into 'houses' and each given a specific aspect of earthly fortunes, such as riches, health, and disaster. Depending on the groupings of the Sun and the planets in these 'houses' at the time of somebody's birth, their future positions at any given time would determine the fortunes of those born under these signs. In addition, great cosmic events, such as comets, were held to foretell terrible disasters on earth.

Ptolemy was the greatest astronomical and geographic genius of his time. His detailed astronomical studies and astrological predictions were revered for 1,400 years as a faultless factual guide to the heavens and the fates of men. In European history, one cosmic incident alone, in 1066, reinforced the teachings of Ptolemy to the point where they were accepted beyond question. A great comet flared across the sky, and the astrological descendants of Ptolemy predicted with certainty that a king would die and the history of the world would change. It certainly did. A few months later Harold, King of Saxon England, was killed in the Battle of Hastings, and England became ruled by the Normans. The great founder of astrology, it seemed, had got the whole thing exactly right.

Ptolemy, however, had, in fact, got it wrong — just about as wrong as you could possibly get. His whole theory had been founded on one gigantic mistake, a cosmic blunder made by every astronomer and astrologer until Polish astronomer Nicolaus Copernicus published his great work, *The Orbits of Celestial Bodies*, in the year of his death, 1543. Ptolemy had stated categorically that the Sun and planets brought their influence to bear on mankind because they revolved around the Earth, the centre of the Universe. Copernicus, on the other hand, proved that the entire work of astronomy and astrology had been based on a totally wrong assumption. In reality, all the planets revolved around the Sun; the Earth was just another one of these planets.

Copernicus's discovery should have sounded the death knell of astrology. Not a bit of it. One hundred and forty years later, the English Astronomer Royal, Edmund Halley, proved by scientific observation that the 1066 comet which preceded the death of King Harold orbited the Sun and came around every 75 years like clockwork, regardless of any trivial events taking place here on Earth.

This should have been another nail in the coffin of astrology, but ironically, it was the work of Halley's great friend and contemporary, Isaac Newton, that gave a boost of bogus feasibility to astrology. Newton's research outlined, for the first time, the laws of gravitational motion. It explained about the forces that gravity exerts on the Sun, the Earth and the planets, and demonstrated how the pull of the Sun and Moon causes the tidal ebbs and flows of oceans.

Astrologers insisted that if far-flung planets could exert gravitational influences on the distant Earth, surely they could affect the personalities of the people of Earth?

But, in actual fact, it has been demonstrated time and time again that the gravity of the planets is so small as to be immeasurable.

With all the scientific evidence serving to debunk astrology, it is difficult to understand why it has persisted with such a dominant, all-pervading grip on the minds of men. Britain's wartime leader, Winston Churchill, was shrewd enough to employ an astrologer to advise him what effects the star signs were having on Adolf Hitler, an avid believer in astrology. Churchill, himself a sceptic about the ancient myth, believed that the study of astrology could give him a valuable insight into the mind of a vulnerable, superstitious enemy such as the German Dictator.

In the Middle Ages, every king, count, and Holy Roman Emperor had their own court astrologer, and Queen Elizabeth I used her astrologer, John Dee, as a personal adviser, military tactician and her first secret service agent, to spy on her enemies. William Lilley, the 17th-century astrologer who predicted the Fire of London and the Great Plague, became astral adviser to both Charles I and the Puritan religious zealot, Oliver Cromwell. In more modern times, few political leaders have been willing to admit that they have sought astrological guidance. However, President 'Teddy' Roosevelt never made any secret of his belief. He even kept a copy of his personal chart on the wall of his White House office and consulted it regularly. And British political leader David Steel admits to having had a personal chart drawn up when he was 17 which, he says 'has since proved uncannily accurate'.

Hollywood millionaire astrologer Carroll Righter, who died in 1988, was a major influence on the lives and careers of powerful and important people in American showbusiness and politics. For example, as an unknown struggling actor, film star Robert Mitchum worked as an assistant to Righter, helping him to cast horoscopes and predictions for many of the influential clients at Righter's astrological consultancy. Mitchum's own career took off shortly after his association with the astrologer. Whether this was through Righter's guidance or simply through meeting important film executives at the astrologer's home, Mitchum has never revealed.

The new breed of astrologers do not need to spend hours poring over charts of astronomical data as their predecessors did, plotting the exact position of the planets in the heavens at the moment of the births of their subjects. Now, armed with expensive computers, they can perform the most intricate calculations in fractions of a second, producing detailed print-outs of astrological predictions.

It is not just in the quest for heavenly guidance in personal relationships that astrologers are consulted. More and more business concerns are seeking the advice of astrologers when it comes to choosing key personnel for important jobs. For example, London employment agency executive Anita Higginson admitted: 'I look at people's star signs to discover certain characteristics, but I've never heard of people being recruited simply because they were born under the right star sign. We find that many of our front-line sales people are either Aries or Sagittarius because they are high profile communicators and leaders, although they can be impulsive.'

Insurance broker Trevor Thwaite offered the top jobs in his Nottingham-based organization to applicants who were born under the star signs he considers most effective. He explained: 'I have made a serious study of birth signs to judge the best zodiac indicators of people who make the best sales staff.' Thwaite's choices were: Gemini: those born under this sign are reckoned to be smooth-tongued and can often talk reluctant customers into signing business contracts; Leo: also good talkers with excellent powers of persuasion; Sagittarius: hard-working and dedicated, they make determined salespeople who won't take no for an answer.

In a survey of Wall Street financial advisers, in testimony presented to a Washington Senate investigation, it was revealed that nearly half of the financial directors in the investment world regularly consult astrologers before they make any decisions.

But it is in the delicate area of global politics and diplomacy that the revelations of contacts with astrology have led to an outcry. Winston Churchill was not the only astute politician to exploit the reliance of many world leaders on astrology. In the '50s and '60s, American CIA spy chiefs, always anxious to penetrate the policy-making sessions of potentially vulnerable governments, compiled their own list of world political leaders who took astrological advice. Through bribes and blackmail, they planted their own 'tame' astrologers in many political circles, including the governments of Mr Mehmet Shehu, Prime Minister of Albania, President Sukarno of Indonesia and Kwame Nkrumah, President of Ghana. One former CIA official admitted that they were able to steer the policies of these governments by inventing astrological guidance that was passed on by their own fortune tellers to unsuspecting presidents and prime ministers. Agents credit fake astrological predictions with avoiding a bloody civil war in Ghana, when President Nkrumah's astrologer was persuaded to advise him to pay a state visit to China. A bloodless coup was carried out in his absence.

However, the CIA have been powerless to prevent their own presidents consulting the stars. Ronald Reagan was one of the most superstitious US presidents of all time, never carrying less than five lucky charms in his pockets when he went to important policy meetings or disarmament negotiations. In his own autobiography, published in 1965 before he became Governor of California, Mr Reagan revealed the reliance he and his wife placed on astral predictions. Paying tribute to Hollywood astrologer Carroll Righter, he wrote: 'Every morning Nancy and I turn to see what he has to say.'

Although his own official biographies give his date of birth as 6 February 1911, the former President always refused pointblank to reveal the exact time, to prevent his rivals casting a precise horoscope and gaining an advantage on him. On his election as Governor, he came in for bitter criticism from state officials when, after taking advice from an astrologer, he decided his official inauguration ceremony should take place at precisely 10 minutes past midnight on 2 January 1967.

But the predictions of Carroll Righter failed to notify the Reagans of the assassination attempt on the President in 1981. After this, Mrs Reagan switched her allegiance to San Francisco astrologer Mrs Joan Quigley, whose White House horoscopes ruled the schedule of President Reagan for the rest of his term.

News of the Reagans' dependence on astrology came from former White House official Donald Regan. The ex-Chief of Staff in Washington had to liaise with Mrs Nancy Reagan to prepare the President's diary, and he claims the schedule was constantly altered and rearranged while Mrs Reagan consulted Mrs Quigley by telephone 3,000 miles away in San Francisco. After the news of Regan's revelations broke, Mrs Quigley explained: 'I'm a serious scientific professional. Mrs Reagan wanted to know if certain actions could be carried out at a safe time and I certainly advised her on that. Astrology is a complicated process, which the layman would have difficulty understanding. I always consult my astrological tables in my book, *The Ephemeris*, to allow me to find the correct relationships of the planets, the Sun and the Moon.'

Mrs Quigly said of the revelations: 'I resent the circus atmosphere surrounding this whole thing. I feel awful. I have never divulged the names of my clients or talked about my business. But I can assure you that a horoscope can tell you more about yourself than hours on a psychiatrist's couch.' Meanwhile, White House official Donald Regan complained: 'At one point I kept a colour-coded diary on my desk, with numerals highlighted in different inks, to remind myself when it was propitious to move the President of the United States from one place to another, or schedule him to speak in public, or commence negotiations with a foreign power.'

The news of Mrs Reagan's consultation with the astrologer caused an immediate alarm within the upper echelons of the CIA, who knew from their own experience how fake astrological advice can sway the policies of the leaders of nations. Their main concern was that Mrs Reagan's calls to San Francisco, made on open telephone lines from the White House and the Presidential retreat at Camp David, had been intercepted by KGB agents and then passed on to Russian leader Mikhail Gorbachev and his military advisers. With Mrs Reagan confiding over the telephone the President's exact schedule while she sought cosmic guidance for him, the Russians could eavesdrop on the most intimate details of his appointments system. They could hear the President's wife reveal all his moods and plans and, armed with the knowledge of the kind of stellar predictions being passed on to the White House, the KGB would know how to exploit the President's weaknesses and indecisions for their own purposes.

When the Intelligence chiefs asked FBI agents to visit Mrs Quigley's apartment in San Francisco on 5 May 1988 for an interview about the secrets she had discussed with Mrs Reagan, the astrologer could not be located. She had already fled from California to the safety of France, after her astrological charts had shown that a line-up of planets would exert such severe gravitational pull on the Earth that San Francisco and large parts of California would be destroyed by earthquakes, as she believed had been predicted by the prophet and mystic Nostradamus. Mrs Quigley returned some time later to find California still intact, but President Reagan's reputation as a careful, reasoning political leader was in tatters.

Despite scepticism about the value of astrology, very little scientific research has gone into answering one of our oldest mysteries: can the stars control our personalities and foretell our future? One meticulous independent study was conducted in the 1970s by French psychologist and statistician Michel Gauquelin, who made a survey of the birth signs of prominent members in different professions. In straightforward, statistical analysis, Gauquelin found that links between people's professional abilities, in business, politics, sport or the arts, and their zodiac birth signs were mathematically far greater than they would be according to chance. Convinced that he had established a clear scientific case for the powers of astrology, he expanded his area of research by offering free, detailed personal horoscopes to the first 1,000 applicants who fitted a random cross-section of the population.

As an experiment, Gauquelin sent each one of his unsuspecting applicants exactly the same personal horoscope, regardless of their zodiac signs. Ninety per cent of them replied, saying they had recognized their personal character-istics immediately, and assuring him that his astrological observations were pinpoint accurate. Eighty five per cent of their spouses also wrote to confirm that the horoscope had exactly captured the personality of their partner.

Dismayed, Gauquelin went back to the drawing board. For he had sent his delighted applicants the same personal zodiac profile – that of a convicted mass murderer!

The Banshee

The noise often begins as a low, wailing sound, a sad, mournful, sobbing cry. Then it rises to a wild, agonized shriek, a piercing, blood-curdling scream. Finally it dies away, fading into a soft, stifled lament. Sometimes, it can be the faint sound of muffled drums, beating out a sombre rhythm, often accompanied by a melancholy dirge on a pipe or flute. It is the sound of the banshee, the spirit which proclaims approaching death. The banshee is a ghostly figure, common in both Scottish and Irish myth, signalling that the end is near.

The word itself is derived from Gaelic 'bean shidhe', and means literally the woman of the fairies. But her purpose is far from the innocent enchantment of fairy myth. In Irish legend, the banshee usually takes the form of the spectre of a woman, brushing her hair and singing her song of mourning outside the family home of those about to die. But the song of death is never heard by the doomed person whose time has come. In Scottish myth, the banshee may appear as an old washerwoman, a solitary 'red fisherman', a headless horseman or simply the sound of an unseen drummer and piper playing a funeral march.

In Irish legend the banshee normally remains unseen and unheard as a form of guardian angel, watching over the members of great aristocratic families, guiding them away from danger and performing the last rites of 'keening' for them as death approaches. According to folklore, only the most privileged of families are protected by being haunted by a banshee. The spirit cannot express itself during a lifetime of guarding a favoured mortal, but can sound a wail of grief when its task is over, just before the moment of death, when its mortal charge is about to be taken from it.

One of the best authenticated instances of the wail of the banshee is the ghostly sound that echoed around the tiny village of Sam's Cross in the south-west of Ireland on 22 August 1922. The villagers had been aware of the comings and goings of fast convoys of cars carrying armed men. One of these men was Michael Collins, head of the Irish Government and Irish Army, who was touring military outposts besieged by rebel forces during Ireland's bloody civil war. Fearful of becoming embroiled in the conflict, the villagers stayed indoors until Collins and his bodyguard had passed through their tiny hamlet, heading back towards the town of Cork. As the sounds of car engines died away, the villagers heard another noise drifting on the wind. It was the wailing scream of the banshee. Then the noise died away. In the chill silence of the late summer evening, few of them could even discern the sound of gunfire on a quiet country road on the outskirts of the village. But they didn't need to listen to the noise of battle to know that the death of an important figure was about to take place.

Next morning, the villagers heard the news, which came as no surprise to them. Michael Collins had been killed by a bullet to the head in an ambush, only a few minutes after they had heard the wail of the banshee.

Psychic researcher Frank Smyth, who has carried out his own study of the myth, reports that the folklore of the banshee has even crossed the Atlantic in the wake of the millions of Irish emigrants who settled in the United States. The descendant of one Irish family, Boston businessman James O'Barry, described to Smyth how he first heard the banshee in Massachusetts as a small boy in the 1930s.

'I was lying in bed one morning,' said O'Barry, 'when I heard a weird noise, like a demented woman crying. It was spring and outside the window

The banshee's mournful wail is a sign that the end is near.

the birds were singing, the sun was shining and the sky was blue. I thought for a moment or two that a wind had sprung up, but a glance at the barely stirring trees told me this was not so. I went down to breakfast and there was my father sitting at the kitchen table with tears in his eyes. I had never seen him weep before. My mother told me that they had just heard by telephone that my grandfather had died in New York. Although he was an old man he was as fit as a fiddle and his death was unexpected.'

It was only some years later that O'Barry was told the legend of the banshee and it was then that he recalled quite clearly hearing the noise on the death of his grandfather.

In 1946 while serving as an officer in the United States Army Air Force in the Far East, O'Barry was awakened by the low howl of the banshee once more. He recalled: 'It was 6 a.m. and this time I was instantly aware of what it was. I sat bolt upright in bed and the hair on the back of my neck prickled. The noise got louder, rising and falling like an air-raid siren. Then it died away and I realized that I was terribly depressed. I knew my father was dead. A few days later I got notification that this was so.'

On one more occasion O'Barry heard the wail of the banshee, as he sat up in bed reading newspapers in his hotel room in Toronto during a business trip. He feared it signalled the death of his wife or his young son or his brothers, but he was strangely reassured that it was none of them. Only later that day, 22 November 1963, did he hear about the assassination in Dallas, Texas, of a close family friend – President John F Kennedy.

In Scottish legend the messenger of death takes on different forms. Folklore on the Isle of Mull claims that, during a family feud, the 16th-century chieftain Ewan was preparing to fight against his father-in-law, the MacLaine of Moy Castle, and was greeted on the eve of battle by an old woman washing a bundle of bloodstained shirts in a cold island stream. He knew she was a messenger of death, and next day he galloped into battle aware that he was going to die. Ewan was killed with one blow from an axe, severing his head from his body. The present clan chieftains maintain that the sight of a headless rider galloping across the hills of Mull is now the new messenger of death, taking over from the ghostly washerwoman.

In the north-east of Scotland, on Tayside, death in the Airlie clan is heralded by the sound of a drummer, whose eerie beat was heard three times in the last century foretelling the death of three members of the family in the next 40 years. In the 1840s the drummer sounded his warning in the home of the Ogilvie family, the chieftains of Airlie, at Cortachy castle, to warn of the death of the Countess. After her death, the Earl remarried and, in 1848, he threw a dinner party which included Miss Margaret Dalrymple as a guest. At the dinner table Miss Dalrymple remarked on the sounds of drums and a fife she had heard from the courtyard while she had dressed. The Earl and the new Countess paled.

The following morning Miss Dalrymple's maid, Ann Day, was clearing her mistress's bedroom wardrobe when she heard the sounds of the drummer in the courtyard below. When she realized the yard was empty, she became quite hysterical.

A day later Miss Dalrymple heard the drummer again and cut short her visit to Cortachy Castle. A few weeks later Lady Airlie died in Brighton, on the south coast of England, leaving behind a despondent note saying she believed the drums had been an omen of her impending death.

Several of the estate workers at Cortachy reported hearing the drums again, in 1853, shortly before the death of the heartbroken Earl. And in 1881, two relatives staying at the Castle heard the drums sound once more. They waited for a sudden and certain death, but the next few days passed uneventfully. It took more than a week for the news to reach them of the death of David Ogilvy, the 10th earl of Airlie, 4,000 miles away in America.

For the Celtic people of Ireland, Scotland and Wales, the legend of the messenger of death is not some remote historic figment of the imagination. In October 1966, when a towering coal-tip in the Welsh valleys became waterlogged and slipped, burying a primary school at Aberfan and killing 116 children and 28 adults, it was preceded by a strange howling noise. The headmaster, Mr Kenneth Davies, described it as a sound 'like a jet plane screaming low over the school in the fog'.

In 1988, in the modern world of high technology, a low screech began to wail out across the North Sea, rising to a deafening scream shortly before the deaths of more than 160 workers aboard the oil rig platform Piper Alpha. Less than a minute later, the platform erupted into a deadly fireball. Experienced engineers who examined the wreckage later came to the conclusion that the noise was caused by high pressure gas escaping from a relief valve as the disaster was about to strike the crew of the oil rig. However, one of the survivors had his own description of the awesome scream, which sounded shortly before his mates died in the icy waters of the North Sea. Rig fitter Derek Ellington, 45, from Aberdeen, explained simply: 'It sounded like the wail of the banshee.'

Voodoo

The shuffling group of nine farm labourers who presented themselves for work in the fields of the plantations of HASCO, the Haitian–American Sugar Corporation, were a sorry sight. They wore ragged clothes, worse than the tattered clothing of most other poor Haitian peasants, and they stood around in sullen silence while orders for gathering in the crops were issued to all the other labour gangs. But that year, 1918, there was a record harvest of sugar cane in the Caribbean republic of Haiti, and the HASCO manager needed all the hands he could find to work in the plantation.

The manager listened patiently to the explanation of village headman Ti Joseph and his wife Constance, who told him the labourers were from a remote part of the mountain area near Haiti's border with the Dominican Republic, and they were shy and nervous because they only spoke their own obscure dialect. The men couldn't understand French or the local Creole language, said Joseph, but if they were kept away from other workers, as a group on their own, they would prove to be tireless and efficient labourers.

Ti Joseph, like most other contract labour negotiators, agreed a rate of pay, to be handed over to him and shared with his team of labourers. The HASCO foreman agreed to give this morose group of villagers an opportunity to prove they were worth their wages. By the end of the day Ti Joseph's group had harvested the biggest quota of sugar cane, stopping only at sunset for a simple meal of unsalted millet porridge. For the rest of the week, the gang of labourers worked uncomplainingly in the sweltering heat and humidity, toiling in the fields, having only one plain meal in the evening, and earning valuable bonuses for their village headman.

On Sunday they rested as work stopped for the day, and the headman left them in the care of his wife, while he travelled to the capital of Port au Prince to spend some of the money he had made from the sweat of the labourers. His wife Constance took pity on the harvesters and escorted them to a local village for a small break from their toils, watching the spectacle of a church festival. But the workers stood around awkwardly and silently, showing no signs of joining in the festivity. Finally, Constance bought them all a treat, a packet of sweet biscuits made of brown sugar and salted nuts. The effect on the workers was dramatic. Chewing on the salted biscuits, they began to cry and wail. Then they staggered off into the mountains and headed back towards their village.

There they were greeted by relatives and friends who reeled back in horror. The sugar plantation labour gang were local men who had been buried in the village graveyard over the past few months. They were, in fact, zombies!

The tale of the zombie workers was published by American writer and explorer William Seabrook who settled in Haiti in the 1920s. His amazing report served only to confirm other ghastly tales of the gruesome occult practices on Haiti, the birthplace of the voodoo black magic cult and the graveyard of the zombies, the living dead. The mysterious practice of voodoo, which had, ironically, helped the black slaves of Haiti win their independence, turned against them to become a haunting oppression. And the zombie warriors, who fought tirelessly to defeat their colonial masters, had become pathetic ghouls trapped in a twilight world between life and death.

Until 1844, the territory of Haiti had occupied the entire mountainous mass of the sprawling island of Hispaniola, the first landing place of Christopher Columbus in his pioneering voyage of discovery to the New World. Originally inhabited by Arawak and then Carib Indians, the history of Hispaniola was first written in blood when the new European explorers embarked on a campaign of slaughter and massacre for the first 50 years after the arrival of Columbus. Hispaniola became a Spanish colony, and almost a

A Haitian woman said to be a genuine zombie.

desert island, after the extermination of the Indians, until it was repopulated by African slaves shipped from across the Atlantic. The unfortunate Africans, wrenched from their homes to work as slave labourers in the fields, brought with them only a few relics of their own culture. But they also brought an unquenchable belief in the African rituals of magic and the occult, which was to grow to become Haiti's own voodoo religion.

In the power struggles which followed, the island of Haiti was eventually ceded to the French, who built up their own repressive, but thriving, economy based on African slave labour and the crops of sugar, coffee and cotton. By the time of the French Revolution in 1789, there were 40,000 Frenchmen in Haiti, controlling a middle class of 30,000 mulattos of mixed race, and more than half a million slaves living in bondage and poverty. The new Emperor, Napoleon Bonaparte, had high hopes of using Haiti as a launching pad for a great naval fleet to recapture France's lost territories in North America. But for the black slaves, who had caught a glimpse of the freedom the French had won for themselves in the overthrow of their own royal masters back in France, their goal was independence from France.

In their bid to break free from oppression, the slaves were led by a mysterious priest and witch doctor, Boukman, who initiated rebellious slaves into voodoo rituals in the deep forests and sent them into battle against the French. Inspired by voodoo ritual and 'magic potions' which robbed them of the fear of pain or death, the black 'zombie' warriors staged a series of uprisings, in which they repaid the brutality of their French rulers with even more appalling savagery of their own. Eventually, under the leadership of General Toussaint l'Ouverture, they triumphed and declared an independent republic, although General l'Ouverture himself was to die in exile and captivity in France.

The new republic struggled into the 20th century, still beset by civil war and instability, with intervention by the French and the British until finally, from 1915 to 1934, it came under rule by the United States. During the 1940s and 1950s there were a series of *coups d'état* until a wily physician, Dr Francois Duvalier, seized power in 1957.

For Duvalier, known throughout Haiti as 'Papa Doc', the ancient religion of voodoo provided a powerful tool for unifying the people of Haiti in the belief that they all shared a unique, cultural bond unknown anywhere else in the world. When his rule degenerated into a cruel dictatorship in 1964, and he declared himself President for Life, voodoo and the mysterious myth of the zombie were enlisted as weapons to cow his people into a life of ignorance and supersition.

Duvalier gave himself the trappings of a high priest of voodoo and surrounded himself with a band of secret policemen, the Tonton Macoutes, meaning 'bogeymen'. The Tonton Macoutes revelled in their fearsome image as part state police and part witch doctors. Papa Doc encouraged voodoo worship, and terrifying tales were spread of the demonic powers of him and his henchmen, saying that anyone who opposed them would be turned into mindless zombies.

Soon the life of the country was completely governed by voodoo and black magic. Haitian peasants concocted bizarre rituals to prevent their dead loved ones from being raised from the grave as zombies. They insisted that their own families should take the same precautions for them on their death to ensure that they were not resurrected as living dead. The terror of villagers was heightened by documented examples of dead relatives, discovered years after their burial, alive but mentally deranged. Even the poorest peasants borrowed money to buy heavy ornate stones to place over the graves of dead relatives, in order to prevent voodoo doctors from digging them up and regenerating them as living ghosts. Bereaved families would take it in turns to watch over fresh graves for several weeks, until they were sure that the body inside was sufficiently decomposed as to be useless to voodoo witch doctors. In other cases, corpses were injected with deadly poisons, mutilated with knives and axes, and riddled with bullets to make sure they stayed dead.

These gruesome practices were actively promoted and encouraged by Duvalier, who needed a pervading atmosphere of fear and witchcraft to keep his grip on the population. But it soon provoked a reaction of disgust from abroad. In 1962, President Kennedy threatened to cut off any more foreign aid from the US to Haiti unless Duvalier introduced democratic measures. Papa Doc reacted angrily by declaring he had put a voodoo curse on the President. In fact, when President Kennedy was assassinated the following year, Duvalier claimed perverted 'credit' for his death and reinforced his power over the people of Haiti still further.

But even witch doctors who practise voodoo are not immortal. In 1971, Francois Duvalier died and his nervous people waited several weeks to make sure he would not rise again as a zombie. Then his son, Jean-Claude, just 19 years old, was installed as President and immediately nicknamed 'Baby Doc'. Western leaders watched closely to see if Haiti, virtually closed to outsiders for three decades, would become a modern democratic society. Their hopes were dashed as 'government by magic' continued under the regime of Baby Doc Duvalier.

In the meantime, another American President had grown impatient with the cruel injustices of the Haitian dictatorship. President Jimmy Carter, ignoring the voodoo curse which was apparently laid on Kennedy, announced that he, too, would retract aid to Haiti if the Duvalier family did not make moves towards granting Haitians basic human rights. In February 1978

Carter himself became the subject of a voodoo curse. The widow of Papa Doc, 'Mama Doc' Duvalier, summoned the Tonton Macoutes and a voodoo priest to a gory ritual in the capital, Port au Prince, where a pit was dug and a live bull was buried, together with a portrait of President Carter. The following year Iranian fanatics stormed the US embassy in Tehran, and when President Carter mounted a rescue effort, US special forces were bogged down in sudden sandstorms in the Iranian desert and many died in collisions involving their own aircraft. Carter was defeated in his attempt to win another term in the White House and left office a bitter and broken man.

Only two years later, a Harvard scientist, Dr E Wade Davis, who had managed to penetrate the veil of secrecy surrounding the voodoo practices in Haiti, announced: 'Zombie-ism actually exists. There are Haitians who have been raised from their graves and returned to life.'

Dr Davis had been recruited specially to study zombies by Dr Lamarque Douyon, the Canadian-trained head of the Port au Prince Psychiatric Centre. The two doctors carried out physical and mental examinations of 'recovered zombie' Clairvius Narcisse, who was declared dead at the Albert Schweizer Hospital in Port au Prince in 1962 but who reappeared alive in his home village two years later.

Narcisse was able to point to the scar on his cheek made by one of the nails driven into his coffin, and had astonished villagers by leading them to his own grave and digging it up to show them the empty coffin. According to Narcisse, he was 'killed' by his brothers for refusing to go along with their plan to sell off part of their family land. He could not recall how long he had been buried, but he was eventually unearthed by a witch doctor who cast a spell on him, which brought him back to life.

Another zombie studied by the doctors, a woman named Ti Femme, had been poisoned by her parents for refusing to marry the husband they had chosen for her and for bearing another man's child.

Dr Davis decided that both Narcisse and Ti Femme had been victims of a rare form of suspended animation, induced by the poison of a voodoo priest. The poison, he explained, is not fatal if administered in precisely the correct dose, but it can give all the convincing symptoms of death. He reported: 'Zombies are a Haitian phenomenon which can be explained logically. The active ingredients in the poison are extracts from the skin of the toad *Bufo marinus* and one or more species of puffer fish. The skin of the toad is a natural chemical factory which produces hallucinogens, powerful anaesthetics and chemicals that affect the heart and nervous system. The puffer fish contains a deadly nerve poison called tetrodotoxin.'

Dr Davis had compared the clinical reports of Haitian zombies with cases in Japan where people had suffered acute poisoning as a result of eating puffer fish from which the tetrodotoxin had not been completely removed. The Japanese case histories, he found, '...read like classic accounts of Haitian zombification'. In at least two cases Japanese victims had been declared dead, but had recovered before their funerals were held.

'A witch doctor in Haiti is very skilled in administering just the right dose of poison,' Dr David explained. 'Too much poison will kill the victim completely and resuscitation will not be possible. Too little and the victim will not be a convincing corpse.'

With the mystery of voodoo and zombies apparently solved, Baby Doc Duvalier's power over the people of Haiti dissolved virtually overnight. In 1986, he fled from his palace at Port au Prince to political asylum in France. Just to make sure that the junior dictator never returns to Haiti, a committee of witch doctors met in the capital and declared a curse on him. Regardless of the scientific evidence of Dr Davis, the witch doctors have warned that if Baby Doc sets foot in Haiti again, he will be turned into a zombie.

The curse seems to have worked so far.

King Arthur

The legend of King Arthur and his Knights of the Round Table is one of the most enduring myths in British folklore. The tales of Arthur's great victory to save his Celtic people from the invading Saxons, of his benevolent rule from his court at Camelot, and of his noble religious piety enthralled and inspired medieval England. He was called the 'once and future' King, and the myth was embellished with the promise that Arthur would return from his resting place on the Island of Avalon to protect Britain if she was ever again threatened by foreign invasion.

European folklore is peppered with mythical promises of sleeping monarchs who will be revived to save nations in time of peril, from Charlemagne, the King of the Franks, to Barbarossa, Frederick I of Germany, and the greatest of Irish heroes, Fionn McCumhaill. But of all the 'slumber kings', the tale of Arthur is so vivid that many historians believe it may actually have some historical authenticity.

MYTH OR FACT?

There seems little doubt that there was, around the 5th century, a great chieftain, possibly a Romanized Briton, who turned the tide against the onslaught of the Saxon occupiers who were plundering the British countryside. Medieval scholars believe the character of King Arthur may be based on the real-life figure of a professional soldier, Ambrosius Aurelianus, who fought bravely against the invasion.

Certainly the battle-weary peasants of Britain were sorely in need of a national hero when the retreat of the Roman legions left them vulnerable and leaderless after centuries of colonial government. By AD 410 Britain, at least south of the Scottish border and the protective ramparts of Hadrian's Wall, had enjoyed 400 years of relative peace, prosperity and the protection of the Roman Army. A network of perfectly engineered roads had provided a sound infrastructure for trade and commerce, as well as allowing Roman legions to move quickly between their encampments and major cities. A well-oiled system of firm central government was another of the benefits imposed on backward Britain by its Roman masters. But when Rome itself was threatened by strife and plundering hordes of barbarians, Emperor Honorius had to pull his troops back to Italy and leave the Britons to fend for themselves. No sooner had the Romans left than Britain was plunged into civil war, prey to rival armies of warlords who saw rich pickings left behind by the enforced retreat of the former colonial masters.

The tyrant Vortigern managed to grab the most widespread power by reinforcing his own band of crude soldiers with two ruthless men imported from the European continent: the Anglo-Saxon mercenaries, Hengist and Horsa. Not content with being only lieutenants in Vortigern's dictatorship, Hengist and Horsa soon turned on their former allies, and Vortigern's regime collapsed in a bloody wave of rioting and looting.

Soon, other marauding bands of Anglo-Saxon private armies crossed the Channel to carve out their own share of the spoils, and the original inhabitants of Britain began to long for the return of the Roman conquerors.

But salvation was at hand in the form of a little known British general, Ambrosius Aurelianus. Pushed further and further west, towards Wales, the British armies, led by Ambrosius, eventually stood their ground on the battlefield of Mount Badon, around the year 518, and defeated the Saxons. The military mastermind credited with the victory is known only as Arthur. His triumph was said to have been so overwhelming that peace was restored for another 50 years.

Early Welsh scribes quickly made Arthur a 'king of wonders and marvels', and his deeds soon became known throughout Britain.

The *Annales Cambriae*, the Welsh annals written by monks, describe how Arthur fought for three days and nights before achieving victory. Intriguingly, they added the pious detail that Arthur carried 'The Cross of Our Lord Jesus' as a symbol on his battle shield. Another entry in the annals laments the battle of Camlann, in which 'Arthur and Mordred perished and a plague fell upon Britain and Ireland'.

Within the next few centuries, based on a few fragments of historical record, the legend of Arthur took on a life of its own, and grew in depth until it was woven into a rich tapestry of unproveable fact and undeniable fiction. Each retelling of the myth tailored the story to fit neatly into the unique national character of ancient Britons, blending a belief in the powers of magic and wizards with a conflicting faith in Christianity.

Arthur's birth was shrouded in magic and intrigue. His father, Uther Pendragon, King of England, had fallen deeply in love with Ygraine, the wife of his most loyal supporter, Gorlois, Duke of Cornwall. Overcome with lust, Uther persuaded his personal wizard Merlin to give him a potion which transformed him into the double of Gorlois, and he had the Duke killed while he entered Ygraine's bed-chamber in Tintagel Castle, posing as her husband.

The result of Uther's passion was the boy Arthur. The wizard Merlin claimed the infant and sent the baby off to be raised by a knight called Ector until he was 15 years old. On Uther's death there was a great gathering of all the nobility of England in London, and under the watchful eye of Merlin, the dukes and earls were invited to pit themselves against a magical stone, holding an anvil in which a sword, named Excalibur, was embedded.

Engraved on the stone were the words: 'Whosoever pulls this sword from the stone and anvil is the rightful King of England'.

The lords and knights puffed and panted as they tried to pull the sword free, but as soon as young Arthur, ignorant of his royal parentage, grasped the sword firmly, it slipped easily into his grasp.

Arthur was proclaimed King, but it took many years of bitter fighting before his authority was accepted. One of the rebel nobles, Loth of Lothian, grudgingly offered his own beautiful wife, Morgause, to Arthur and the couple conceived a child. Arthur was unaware that Morgause was his own half-sister, a daughter of Gorlois and Ygraine, and Merlin prophesied that the boy who was born of their incest, Mordred, would eventually lead to the downfall of his kingdom.

In later years Arthur remarried, and he and his second wife, Guinevere, established their kingdom in Camelot. Embellishments of the legend spoke of the fabled Round Table, given as a wedding present to Guinevere, where all the Knights of Camelot were seated in a circle without any single person being given a privileged position higher or lower in authority than any other. Only one seat was left vacant, reserved for the brave knight who would one day succeed in the spiritual challenge to locate the Holy Grail, the most

Arthur, Guinevere and Merlin have their roots in real history.

revered relic in Christendom, the chalice used by Jesus Christ to sip wine at the Last Supper.

The Grail was believed to have been brought to England by Joseph of Arimathea, who fled from the Holy Land to escape the persecution of Jews angered by the fact that Jesus's body had been taken to Joseph's tomb after his crucifixion. Ancient legend, probably fuelled by devout religious wishful thinking, also claimed that Jesus himself had spent his early years in England learning the trade of a tinsmith in the West Country, hence the Bible's total lack of reference to the Saviour's early life in Palestine.

Although the adventures of the Knights of the Round table were tales of thrilling bravery, honour and dedication to the highest principles of gallantry, Arthur's own life was shattered by betrayal and dishonour. He lost his beloved wife, Guinevere, to his bravest knight, Sir Lancelot, which broke his heart. Eventually, forced by his ambitious son, Mordred, to publicly accuse the couple of adultery and treason, Arthur watched the break-up of his idyllic Kingdom of Camelot.

Lancelot and Guinevere, accompanied by a band of renegade knights, fled to France and were pursued by Arthur who forced a bloody showdown. Back home in Camelot, Sir Mordred exploited the situation to his own advantage, and when Arthur returned he found his throne had been usurped. Arthur and his loyal knights met Mordred and the rebel forces on the battlefield at Camlann. Amid the carnage and deaths of valiant knights, Arthur struck a mortal blow at his son; and Mordred, with his dying breath, plunged his own sword into Arthur.

The wounded king was taken away to the shores of an enchanted lake and carried off to die in a little chapel built by Joseph of Arimathea on the mystical island of Avalon.

The legend of Arthur had all the ingredients of a best-seller. It satisfied the Britons' hatred and distrust of foreigners by extolling Arthur's victories over invading Saxons. And while it was steeped in magic and sorcery, it also paid devout homage to Christianity. It had passionate romance, adultery, treachery, double-dealing, honour and gallantry in equal measures. And it had an optimistically happy ending, with the tragic but noble figure of the wounded King Arthur being borne to the mystical island of Avalon, promising to return to rescue his beloved people once more in their darkest hour of need.

All in all, the legend of King Arthur was a ripping yarn, and more glorious detail and embellishment was added with each retelling. In AD 1135 a Benedictine monk, Geoffrey of Monmouth, devoted a large part of his massive tome, *The History of the Kings of England*, to King Arthur, presenting his version of events not as legend and myth but as historical fact. Even the Norman rulers of conquered Britain were captivated by the fabulous picture of Arthur portrayed in the book. They saw Arthur as a home-grown hero who was a worthy rival to their own legendary King Charlemagne. And since the Norman invaders had fought and defeated the Saxon rulers of England in their own conquest, they felt this victory over the common enemy of King Arthur gave them some kind of kinship with their new British subjects.

The legends of Arthur were already well known in France at this time, having been carried there by the blood relatives of West Country Britons who settled in the province of Brittany in northern France. At Bayeux, also in France, the cleric Robert Wace rewrote large parts of Geoffrey of Monmouth's *History* with even more poetic licence and embellishment, adding flourishes of detail to the romantic code of chivalry of the Knights of the Round Table. Another Frenchman, Chrétien de Troyes, helped to popularize the tales of Arthur even further with several long epic poems in praise of the honour of Arthur's knights.

The story of King Arthur might have remained no more than a romantic legend but for the discovery of a startling record in the chronicles of Glastonbury Abbey. The Abbey's reputed association with Joseph of Arimathea made it the most logical location for the site of Camelot and the island of Avalon. In Arthurian times the area was surrounded by marshy swamps and streams, effectively making it an island. The Welsh called it Ynys Avallon, meaning the island of apples, and its description dovetailed neatly with the tales of the island where Arthur and his unfaithful Queen Guinevere were eventually buried.

Writing in the 10-year period between 1129 and 1139, historian William Malmesbury described how Arthur's grave was found standing between two stone pyramids in the ancient cemetery of the Lady Chapel of the Abbey. According to Malmesbury, the grave was marked with a cross inscribed with the words: '*Hic jacet sepultus inclitus Rex Arthurus cum Wenneveria uxore sua secona in Insula Avallonis.*' Translated from the Latin, it reads simply: 'Here lies the famous King Arthur with Guinevere, his second wife, buried in the Island of Avalon.'

Malmesbury's reports fit exactly with the Abbey's own records: that Bishop Dunstan raised the level of the cemetery in the 10th century and enclosed it with a wall. It is possible that the grave was discovered then. Abbot Henry of Sully is also reputed to have exhumed the coffin from its burial place 16 feet under the earth in 1190 and transferred it to the Treasury of the Abbey.

Eighty-five years later, King Edward and Queen Eleanor, having heard the tales of Arthur's grave from Welsh bards, journeyed to Glastonbury to celebrate the consecration of the Abbey's High Altar. On the arrival of the monarchs, King Arthur's coffin was broken open to reveal two separate chests, decorated with portraits of Arthur and Guinevere and their heraldic arms. The Queen was shown fully crowned, but Arthur wore a battle-damaged crown. His left ear was cut off and there were marks of his wounds from the battle with Mordred at Camlann. When the caskets were opened the King's bones were found to be those of a tall and powerful man, while those of Guinevere were of a delicate woman.

The following day King Edward and Queen Eleanor reverently wrapped the remains in fresh shrouds, keeping out the bones of King Arthur's skull, and his knees, to display to pious worshippers. The remains were encased in a mausoleum before the High Altar. King Edward then presided over a public ceremony to emphasize that he was the worthy and legitimate successor to King Arthur and rightfully the monarch of all Britain.

In 1960, archaeologists excavated the area where Arthur's tomb was reputed to have been. They found only evidence that a pit had existed there, and there were also the imprints of a stone memorial which had since been removed. The pit had been emptied and refilled at the time of King Edward's visit. It seems that the monks of Glastonbury had exhumed a grave and tried to cover up their traces.

Was it the grave of King Arthur and his Queen? Did the mythical King actually live and fight and love in the days of Camelot? And is his final resting place still undiscovered and undisturbed somewhere in the west of England, in a secret place once known to his Knights as the Island of Avalon?

Glastonbury Abbey

When architect Frederick Bond was given the task of excavating and exploring the ruins of Glastonbury Abbey in Somerset, western England, he faced a seemingly impossible task. Many of its ancient buildings had disappeared completely in the terrible destruction of the Abbey by the soldiers of Henry VIII, and the ravages of time and weather had helped to reduce the few remaining arches and columns of its two main chapels to rubble.

The Abbey had been founded in the 5th century by Saint Patrick before he left England on his mission to convert Ireland to Christianity, and the site had long been associated with the legend of King Arthur. As a popular place of pilgrimage, it had grown in power, wealth and influence under a series of monks and abbots who had enlarged the Abbey grounds and extended the splendour of its architecture. This had made Glastonbury a prime target for revenge by King Henry, who had broken with the Catholic Church over the controversy of his many wives and divorces. Henry ordered the Abbey razed to the ground so thoroughly that when the Church of England finally paid £36,000 for the ruins in 1907, there were few clues left to the exact layout of the ancient place of worship, and there was precious little money to pay for the extensive digging and research needed to piece together the elaborate medieval jigsaw.

The eerie ruins of St Joseph's Chapel, Glastonbury Abbey.

Bond, a leading expert of Gothic architecture and the restoration of old churches, realized that uncovering the remains of the ruined Abbey in the little time and money made available to him would need incredible luck and inspiration. Or divine guidance. The 43-year-old scholarly authority on ancient buildings had one untried gamble he hoped would pay off. But he didn't dare reveal it to the Church dignitaries. He decided, instead, to go 'straight to the horse's mouth' for the information he needed – by contacting the spirits of the long-dead monks and abbots.

Bond was a secret student of the occult, and one of his closest friends was psychic medium John Bartlett, who specialized in receiving messages from the spirit world in the form of 'automatic writing' transmitted to him while in a trance. In a seance at Bond's office in Bristol in November 1907, Bartlett made contact with a disembodied spirit, who guided his pen through a series of notes and drawings tracing detailed plans of the hidden foundations of the ruined abbey.

The messages, which seemed to flow effortlessly from Bartlett's pen, purported to come from a 16th-century monk, John Bryant, who spoke on behalf of the ghostly keepers of the Abbey whom he described as 'The

Company of Avalon'. The information given in these seances contradicted Bond's lifetime of experience of the layout of medieval monasteries, but when he was finally allocated his meagre budget two years later, he decided to direct his workmen to dig in the area where the ghostly writing said they would discover the underground foundations of old chapels and the stone-work of ancient walls.

On the first few weeks of digging, Bond's team, working to the master plan of the dead monk, found walls and towers, doorways and fragments of stained glass windows. Bond's reputation soared as discovery after discovery began to piece together the shattered remains of Glastonbury Abbey. Fearful of the ridicule of fellow professionals and his clerical paymasters, Bond modestly took the credit himself and put his amazing finds down to a piece of inspired guesswork.

Ten years after the excavations had begun, Bond decided to reveal the source of his success, confident that the work he had already done would justify the unorthodox methods he had used. In a dramatic book, *The Gate of Remembrance*, he confessed to the mystic seances that had taken place, and admitted to the messages from the spirit world which had guided the shovels of his archaeological team.

After the publication of *The Gate of Remembrance*, Bond's reputation was left in tatters. A co-director was immediately appointed by the Church authorities to supervise Bond and to edge him out of control of any more excavation work. Within a year, the budget for any further digging under Bond's direction had been slashed, and he was reduced to a salary of only £10 a month.

In 1922, when the dust had settled, the Church society for the exploration and restoration of Glastonbury Abbey was quietly dissolved and Bond was banned from setting foot on the Abbey grounds ever again. He left for America, where he lived for the next 20 years, lonely and embittered. He never got over the deep hurt that Church leaders and fellow archaeologists could not accept his claim that the dead monk of Glastonbury had communi-cated with his colleague Bartlett's subconscious mind and had drawn mental images for him of the original plans of the Abbey.

Alchemy

There are many incentives that spur on scientists, researchers and philosophers to devote their lives to the quest for wisdom and truth. There is the desire for knowledge for its own sake; there are the honourable motives of gaining the ability to advance mankind, to pass on some greater understanding of the mysteries of Life, to enrich society and suceeding generations; and then there's greed, lust for power and the fear of dying.

There is no doubt that the alchemists who sweated over their crucibles and cauldrons made a modest contribution to the progress and understanding of the fledgling sciences of chemistry and metallurgy. But even this was unintentional. The objective of any alchemist who made a worthwhile chemical discovery was to keep the find a secret, to note the formulae and processes in uncrackable codes and ciphers, and to make sure the discovery could be of no benefit to anyone else.

Alchemy only had one purpose: to make its practitioners fabulously rich. There was also the possibility of an added bonus – immortality!

A corruption of the true scientific course of chemistry, the aim of alchemy was to turn base, mundane metals, such as iron, lead and mercury, into gold and silver. To Egyptian priests and chemists in 5,000 BC the idea of turning crude metal ores into the precious commodities must have seemed almost within their grasp. They had already conquered many of the mysteries of metallurgy. They could recognize the distinctive streaks of seams of metal in rocks and earth. They knew how to grind up soil and stone, how to heat the ore in furnaces and skim off bright shiny metals like copper and tin. But it was much more difficult to locate and mine the rare rocks which contained tiny glistening seams of gold, or to find twinkling specks of pure gold nuggets in the beds of rivers and streams.

Gold was not just rare, it was precious. It was soft enough to be moulded and shaped into ornaments of great delicacy and beauty. It seemed like a gift from the gods, and kings counted their power and wealth in the amounts of gold they possessed in their treasury. It could be stamped into coinage, bearing the imprint of a ruler's face, spreading his power and influence far and wide. It never tarnished or rusted, like ordinary metals. It had the aura of immortality and coin-makers thought, maybe, some of that would rub off on a king whose head was stamped into gold.

The Pharaohs, who faced an eternity of death in their pyramid tombs, became more and more frantic to be surrounded with gold as the symbols of their wealth and power. How much easier and richer life would be for all if a plentiful metal like lead or tin could be turned into gold.

The ancient Egyptians knew that something as common as sand mixed with wood ash would be miraculously transformed into tough, translucent sparkling glass, precious and expensive, almost like man-made jewels or diamonds. The secret of changing metals into gold obviously lay in understanding the inner workings of the kind of chemistry that turned sand into glass. So the quest began to find the key to the mystery. Blind to everything except the quest for man-made gold, the alchemists set off on a race without a winning post, a frantic, futile scramble around a chemical treadmill.

The history of alchemy is marked by cheats and charlatans, honest chemists and brilliant scientists, gullible monarchs like Queen Elizabeth I, who squandered a fortune on crack-brained alchemy schemes, and dictators like Adolf Hitler, who partly financed his rise to power with an alchemy swindle.

Generations of the most skilful Egyptian chemists had already seen their best efforts come to nothing by the time conquering warriors swept northward out of the Arabian peninsula in the 7th century AD and occupied the country, introducing Islamic rule. In the great library of Alexandria, the new Arab masters and scholars found a wealth of manuscripts, including the writings of Aristotle, who had lived a thousand years earlier.

According to Aristotle, every compound in the world was made up of only four elements – earth, air, water and fire. And it was only necessary to change the proportions of these components to form any substance. Aristotle's teachings were transcribed into Arabic and carried back across the Mediterranean by Moslem invaders who conquered Spain and established great universities at Toledo and Cordova.

In 1144 an Englishman, Robert of Chester, made the first Latin translation of Aristotle's theories, and Aristotle's faulty chemical formulae became the foundation of a pseudo-science which turned the lives of countless alchemists of the Middle Ages into a fruitless quest for the non-existent answer to the mystery of the transmutation of metals.

In addition to being able to turn base metal into gold, the philosopher Aristotle also held out a promise of the Secret of Eternal Youth. Any alchemist who successfully reduced a metal to its basic components, would find himself with an 'Elixir', possibly a powder or a liquid, which possessed magical properties. This 'Philosopher's Stone' could be taken in a drink, curing all illnesses and bringing the gift of immortality.

From then until the present day, scientists have laboured to convert one element to another, with varying degrees of success. For hundreds of years, in castles and dungeons, alchemists muttered magic words and chemical formulae over bubbling cauldrons, trying unlikely combinations of lead, mercury, sulphur and arsenic to produce gold.

The brilliant 13th-century English scholar Roger Bacon, who, long before Columbus, had reached the scientifically accurate conclusion that the Earth was round, and who constructed early magnifying glasses, was a firm believer in alchemy. He had faith that the mystery would be solved sooner or later by thorough and detailed experimentation. He died frustrated and bitterly disappointed that alchemy had not been proved practical during his own lifetime.

Impatient with the slow progress of her officially approved buccaneers who plundered Spanish galleons sailing back from America, where they themselves had already looted Inca gold, Elizabeth I employed her own alchemist in a specially constructed laboratory in Somerset House, London. The alchemist laboured day and night to conquer the mysteries of making gold. Elizabeth dreamt of untold wealth, and of extending her reign indefinitely by sipping of the Elixir of Life. She lived to the ripe old age of 70, and the unsuccessful chemist lived out the rest of his days imprisoned in the Tower of London.

Ferdinand III, the 17th-century Emperor of Austria, was confident that alchemy would finance his victory in the Thirty Years' War against the Germans, Dutch and Swedes, when his Royal Alchemist produced brilliant nuggets of gold from a glowing furnace he had fed with lead and sulphur. Ferdinand was eventually forced to sue for peace when his empire was bankrupted. There is no record of the fate of the alchemist, but he was undoubtedly one of the many rogues and charlatans who saw rich rewards in alchemy, not by manufacturing gold, but by combining a blend of chemistry, magic and occultism to cheat his royal patron.

Clever conjuring tricks were used to fool the gullible. Apparently empty metal cauldrons were secretly lined with a layer of wax, concealing tiny nuggets of gold which were released into the boiling mixtures when they were poured over them, melting the wax. Hollow wands containing gold dust were used to stir the cauldrons and sprinkle flecks of real gold into bubbling broths of cheap metals.

The disillusioned Swiss physician and alchemist Paracelsus, who died in 1541, had tried to put a stop to the practice of alchemy, claiming that it was consuming too much of the talent and limited research facilities of early chemists. Celebrating his appointment as physician to the city of Basle, he burned the written works of earlier alchemists in a bonfire in the city square and urged scientists to abandon their search for manufactured gold and to concentrate on improving their research into medicines.

Frenzied alchemists at work, as depicted by Pieter Brueghel.

Modern scientific methods and knowledge should have finally finished off the ancient myth of alchemy when nuclear physics began to unravel the mysteries of the atom. Instead, they gave alchemy an unexpected boost when, in 1919, British physicist Ernest Rutherford shook the scientific world with the announcement that he had successfully changed one element into another. He had changed nitrogen into oxygen and hydrogen. He had not used any secret chemical processes or added any 'elixir' to the nitrogen gas sample in his laboratory, but had simply bombarded the nitrogen with radiation from the nuclei of helium particles. This transformed it to fluorine, as an intermediate element, before its final conversion into oxygen and hydrogen.

Rutherford's pioneering work was as uneconomic as it was radical. It had taken massive amounts of energy to produce only a few atoms of oxygen, but it had proved a fundamental scientific principle. It had finally shown that elements could be changed, even if it was not through the magical, mystical processes of alchemy.

Five years after Rutherford's breakthrough, a 36-year-old chemical worker in Munich, Franz Tausend, claimed that he had achieved the same atomic transformation, not by turning nitrogen into oxygen, but by turning iron oxide and quartz into gold. Tausend published a pamphlet, asserting that atomic nuclei were held together by vibrating harmonies, and that the frequency of vibration could be altered to produce different elements.

Tausend was greeted with wary cynicism by German scientific authorities, but he was a godsend to the newly formed Nazi Party. In 1924, Adolf Hitler had been sent to jail for plotting an armed uprising against the Government. He left his loyal supporter General Erich Ludendorff in charge of fundraising for the Party. Ludendorff had heard about the claims of Tausend and he gathered together a group of industrialists and investors to give him enough backing to demonstrate that his research really could produce massive profits. At a meeting in a Berlin hotel, one of the business investors was appointed to independently supervise Tausend's exhibition of his alchemic success.

The investor himself bought the supplies of iron and oxide specified by Tausend. The metals were melted together and locked in the impartial referee's hotel room overnight, away from any attempt at interference by the alchemist. The next morning, the solidified mass was reheated by Tausend, under the watchful eyes of his potential backers, and the alchemist added a small quantity of white powder to the molten mixture. When the crucible had cooled down, it was broken open and Tausend produced a gold nugget weighing a quarter of an ounce.

Overnight, investment money began to pour into the coffers of a new company formed as a partnership between Tausend and the officials of the Nazi Party. However, not all the money went to financing Tausend's new laboratory and workshop. Ludendorff managed to divert almost 500,000 marks into the bank accounts of Party funds, and when he resigned from the joint company two years later, he left Tausend to fend off the creditors.

Tausend, without any money for production, struggled for another two years to keep the debt collectors at bay, and on 16 June 1928 he staved off bankruptcy by finally producing an ingot of nearly 26 ounces of gold in one single night.

Faith had been restored in Tausend's methods and the investors who had been howling for his blood rushed to snap up share certificates in his new company. Sadly for trusting investors, that was the last pot of gold produced by the alchemist. In 1931 he was arrested, found guilty of fraud and jailed for four years.

But the future rise to power of the Nazis was secured by the profits of alchemy, and the income from Tausend's bubbling crucible was enough to set them on the road to seizing power in Germany and plunging the world into war only a few years later. And it was the violent course of that war which was to destroy the secret papers of one man who may have unlocked the mystery of alchemy.

London osteopath Archibald Cockren was no crackpot inventor of a secret, magic process for making gold, nor was he seeking to get rich quick by cashing in on alchemy. As part of his respected medical practice, Cockren used small quantities of gold to make medical solutions for the treatment of arthritis. Gold was an increasingly rare commodity during the stringencies of war, so Cockren began to experiment himself in finding a gold substitute – or making the real thing – in his tiny laboratory at home.

Cockren tested the reactions of different metals, including antimony, iron and copper, to which he added a secret catalyst powder capable of sparking off chemical reactions. In 1940 he noted in the brief diary he kept in his office: 'I entered upon a new course of experiment with a metal with which I had no previous experience. This metal, after being reduced to its salts and undergoing special preparation and distillation, delivered up the Mercury of the Philosophers, the Water of Paradise. The first intimation I had of this triumph was a violent hissing, jets of vapour pouring from the retort, like sharp bursts from a machine gun, and then a violent explosion, whilst a very potent and subtle odour filled the laboratory and its surroundings.'

That night he went home to repeat the experiment, and to submit his notes to the War Office. Outside, the air raid wardens were checking the blackout curtains along the street of terraced houses, and then the warning sirens began to wail. It was one of the worst Blitz raids on London, carried out by the bombers of the Nazi regime which, ironically, had been founded on the proceeds of Tausend's dubious experiments.

By the time the all clear signal had sounded, Cockren's house lay in ruins, the osteopath was dead and his research was shattered and burned to ashes.

Alchemy had helped to build up the war machine that destroyed the work of a dedicated researcher, who might actually have solved its mysteries.

Fairies

There can be few people who would not accept that Sir Arthur Conan Doyle, the doyen of detective thriller writers, had a brilliantly sharp, analytical mind. He showed the depth of his talent for unemotional, logical, detached reasoning in the creation of the most enduring character in the history of crime fiction, the formidable Sherlock Holmes. It probably follows, then, that when it came to finding the answer to a mystery or solving a perplexing riddle, Sir Arthur Conan Doyle was as clear-headed and rational as his brainchild, the supersleuth of Baker Street. Like Sherlock Holmes, Sir Arthur was nobody's fool.

Or was he? Did Sir Arthur have the wool pulled over his eyes by two little girls barely into their teens? Was he fooled by a simple trick into believing that the high-spirited, giggling girls had actually photographed fairies at the bottom of their garden?

The photographs, taken by 15-year-old Elsie Wright and her 11-year-old cousin Frances Griffiths, were, apparently, only meant for a family album or as souvenir snapshots to send to friends. In fact, the first print of the photographs which were to become the centre of a furious occult controversy was posted casually to a penfriend along with a chatty letter which only made passing reference to the astonishing picture.

Frances Griffiths, who was living with cousin Elsie while her father fought on the French battlefront in the First World War, had written to a friend in South Africa, where she had spent most of her young life. She told her: 'I am learning French, Geometry, Cookery and Algebra at school now. Dad came home from France the other week after being there ten months and we all think the war will be over in a few days. I am sending two photographs, both of me, one of me in a bathing-costume in our back yard, Uncle Jack took that, while the other is me with some fairies. Elsie took that one. Rosebud is as fat as ever and I have made her some new clothes. How are Teddy and Dolly?'

Frances had scrawled across the back of the photograph: 'Elsie and I are very friendly with the fairies. It is funny I never used to see them in Africa. It must be too hot for them there.'

The photograph showed Frances, nestled on a grassy bank near a beck, a small stream, at the bottom of the garden of the Wright's home in Cottingley, near Bradford, Yorkshire. She had her chin nestled in her cupped

Frances Griffiths with fairies, photographed by Elsie Wright.

hand. In front of her, dancing among the leaves and twigs, was a group of fairies, dressed in gossamer gowns, with wings fluttering. A fairy in the foreground played a set of pipes.

The photograph had been taken more than a year before in July 1917, when Elsie Wright had pestered her father Arthur to borrow his camera for a snapshot of Frances beside the beck that bordered their long, secluded garden. When she returned later that afternoon, her doting father began to develop the photographic plate in his darkroom. As the image appeared, he was annoyed to see what he thought were scraps of litter and old sandwich wrappings on the grass in front of the figure of Frances. Elsie blithely insisted that the white images on the photograph were fairies, and then skipped back outdoors to play.

A few weeks later, the two girls asked again to borrow the camera. They ran off to a clump of trees at the foot of the garden and took another snapshot. This time, when it was developed, Arthur Wright was amazed to see an image of his daughter, seated on the grass, being presented with a tiny flower-bud – by a gnome wearing a doublet, hose and a fancy shirt with a frilled collar. Arthur accused the girls of playing tricks with his precious camera – and he refused to let them borrow it any more. Intrigued by the images, he studied the photographic plates closely, but he could see no signs of hidden strings and wires propping up the fairy figures in front of the lens. He and his wife, Polly, even searched the girls' bedroom, looking for waste paper or scraps of pictures or cutouts which the girls might have used to fake the photographs. They found nothing.

Unsure if he was the victim of a lighthearted prank, or if he had unique, concrete evidence of the fabled creatures of folk myth, Arthur Wright made a few prints to show his neighbours for their novelty value, and thought no more about it.

It wasn't until 1919 that the story of the fairy photographs reached a wider audience. Polly Wright, who had an interest in spiritualism, attended a meeting of the Theosophical Society in Bradford and revealed the existence of the photographs taken by her daughter and her niece. The following year prints of the slightly overexposed photographs were collected by Edward Gardner, a leading member of the Theosophical Society, a society dedicated to exploring psychic phenomena and spreading the message of Spiritualism.

Gardener was fascinated. He ordered photographic expert Fred Barlow to make new copy negatives from the prints, correcting the errors of exposure – but without any touching up or improvements of the actual images. The result was a set of greatly enhanced prints, which showed the girls, the fairies and the gnome with startling clarity.

Even then, the photographs might have remained a curiosity, studied solely by followers of the Theosophist cult. Then: Enter Sherlock Holmes, in the form of Sir Arthur Conan Doyle.

The famous author had been commissioned by *Strand Magazine* in London to write an article on fairies for their Christmas issue. He asked to borrow the prints from Gardner, and showed them to Sir Oliver Lodge, a psychical researcher. Lodge immediately dismissed them as fakes and suggested, bizarrely, that the fairies in the prints might have been a troupe of dancers in disguise, reduced in size by a trick of photographic perspective.

But Sir Arthur, apparently keen to seek a second opinion, gave more credence to a report by a technical expert employed by Edward Gardner, who insisted that his own analysis showed that the fairy figures were not lifeless cardboard cutouts, but actually showed signs of movement captured by the camera's slow shutter speed.

Casting Edward Gardner in the role of 'Watson', Sir Arthur despatched him to Cottingley to conduct his own interviews with the Wright family and their niece. Gardner reported back that the Wrights were honest, reliable people who were plainly telling the truth. That was enough for Sir Arthur; he gave the Cottingley fairy photographs the backing of his considerable reputation and promoted them in his article in *Strand Magazine*.

Sir Arthur seems to have been swayed by the philosophy he himself invented for Sherlock Holmes when berating Dr Watson in the novel *A Study in Scarlet*: 'How often have I said to you, that when you have eliminated the impossible, whatever remains, however improbable, must be the truth.'

But the author had also put different sentiments into the mouth of his sleuth in an earlier novel, when the redoubtable Sherlock Holmes had proclaimed: 'Detection is, or ought to be, an exact science, and should be treated in the same cold and unemotional manner.'

So Sir Arthur hedged his bets.

As the Christmas edition of *Strand Magazine* sold out within days, Sir Arthur asked Gardner to go back to Cottingley, taking with him his own camera and a supply of photographic plates, secretly marked, without the knowledge of Elsie or Frances. He thought that if a new set of fairy photographs could be made, under controlled circumstances, he might have the definitive proof he was looking for. Sir Arthur then promptly departed for a lecture tour of Australia, while a storm of controversy broke out over the report in *Strand*: 'Fairies Photographed, an Epoch Making Event.'

The popular press had a field day. Sir Arthur, who had written under a pseudonym for the magazine article in order to protect the true identities of Frances and Elsie, was lampooned and laughed at. The *South Wales Argus* gave the Cottingley fairies as much credibility as Santa Claus. In London, the *City News* mocked: 'It seems at this point that we must either believe in the almost incredible mystery of the fairy or in the almost incredible wonders of faked photographs.'

The *Westminster Gazette*, however, adopted tactics more worthy of Sherlock Holmes. By following every clue and hint, they cracked the protective aliases used by Sir Arthur, and correctly identified Elsie and Frances. Their staff reporter travelled to Cottingley and conducted a first-hand investigation on the spot. He found no flaws in the story and, grudgingly perhaps, his own report to his paper classified the Cottingley Fairies as 'an unexplained mystery'.

In the meantime, the luckless Edward Gardner had been unsuccesful in his efforts to witness the apparitions of the fairies for himself. It rained in Cottingley for days on end, and the weather was obviously not conducive to fairy dancing and prancing. He therefore left his equipment behind with Elsie and Frances, with instructions to use the camera themselves.

The following month, back in London, he received a letter from Polly Wright, together with five photographic plates that had already been developed. Gardner was gratified to see the secret marks he had already made

Elsie Wright plays with a 'gnome' at Cottingley in 1917.

on the plates, showing that his own material had been used without substitution or tampering. The girls had succeeded in taking three more fairy snapshots. Although no adults had witnessed the event, the unsupervised girls had followed Gardner's instructions about focusing and exposure, and the plates were remarkably clear. One showed a close-up of Elsie being offered a tiny harebell flower by a fairy – who displayed a suspiciously fashionable '20s bobbed hairstyle and flapper dress. A second snapshot showed a prancing fairy in more realistic gossamer dress, flying in the air a few feet from the smiling face of Frances. And a third plate had captured the blurred image of two tiny figures in a 'fairy bower' of blossoms and twigs, shyly adjusting their dresses in the morning dew.

Gardner's unswerving belief was reinforced. He cabled the good news to Sir Arthur in Australia, who replied joyfully: 'My heart was gladdened when I had your note and the three wonderful pictures which are confirmatory of our published results. When fairies are admitted, other psychic phenomena will find a more ready acceptance. We have had continued messages at seances for some time that a visible sign was coming through.'

However, the new photographs failed to convince the sceptics. They even failed to impress Elsie's father, Arthur Wright, a bluff, down-to-earth Yorkshireman. Wright, who believed only in the benefits of education and reasoning, was baffled. He told friends he didn't see how an intellectual like Sir Arthur could be taken in 'by our Elsie, and her at the bottom of her class'.

The hubbub over the Cottingley Fairies soon died away. Decades later, in adulthood, Elsie and Frances still refused to be drawn into any debate about the authenticity of the photographs. The most telling, and ambiguous, verdict on the case was the perhaps the summing up of the newspaper *Truth*, in 1921. It deduced, sarcastically: 'For the true explanation of these fairy photographs what is wanted is not a knowledge of occult phenomena, but a knowledge of children.'

Sir Arthur died in 1930, still clinging to the belief that the folk legend of fairies had been verified as a concrete reality by the apparitions in Cottingley.

There may be some real scientific evidence for the timeless legends of fairies, gnomes and trolls, which are common in many northern European myths. Archeologist A McLean May made an amazing discovery in 1959 when excavating a gravel pit in Ireland – the country which, more than most, had folk myth rich in tales of fairies and leprechauns. Deep under the layers of gravel and clay he found the remains of three distinct civilizations, dating as far back as 7,000 BC He uncovered traces of ovens and cooking fires in tunnels so small they could only have been used by midgets. His research supported the theory that the early inhabitants of the tiny tunnels may have arrived in Ireland soon after the Ice Age, and possibly to other parts of the recently frozen North. The last survivors of the miniature people, now extinct, may have taken to the woods and other hiding places, and glimpses of them by later settlers could have given rise to the legends of the wee folk, the leprechauns of Ireland, the fairies of England and the trolls of Scandinavia.

Whatever the truth, fairy folklore is still strong in Ireland and other parts of the British Isles, including the Isle of Man where the islanders would never dare to pass over the Fairy Bridge of Balla-g-Lonney without bidding a greeting to the fairies and elves. When the cynical servicemen of the RAF station at nearby Jurby ignored the custom, they were warned by the locals: 'The little people will get their own back.' Fliers know all about mysterious 'gremlins', unexplained instances of failure and foul-ups which can plague machinery and aircraft without any apparent cause. But their base was afflicted by a whole series of minor mishaps – cash shipments to pay their wages never arrived on time and military vehicles started seizing up for no apparent reason – whenever they tried to drive over the Fairy Bridge. The problems ceased when the airmen adopted the custom of raising their hats, or saluting smartly, and paying homage to the Fairies of Balla-g-Lonney.

So who says fairies don't exist? The last word should to to Sir Arthur Conan Doyle, or at least his alter ego, the sage of Baker Street, Sherlock Holmes, who said reprovingly to his detractors in *The Memoirs of Sherlock Holmes*: 'You see, but you do not observe.'

Chapter Four

MYSTERIES OF THE MIND

Psychologists, psychiatrists and neurologists have been able to understand much of the workings of the mind. Yet it is still a mystery why some children are born outstanding geniuses, and why people can suddenly regain their memory after years of total amnesia. The work of hypnotists has shown that it is possible to do remarkable things to the mind, and others have given undeniable evidence of out-of-body experiences. Locked inside the human mind is a powerful, and perhaps inpenetrable, web of mystery ...

Child Prodigies

In the 4th century BC the Greek philosopher Plato first tried to identify and channel the potential genius of child prodigies. 'They are the Children of Gold,' he proclaimed. He tried to predict whether they were most likely to have scholarly parents. Plato thought that, detected early enough and encouraged in the study of philosophy and metaphysics, prodigies could change the world in just one generation.

However, there is no predicting where a child prodigy will spring from. He or she may be the son or daughter of aspiring intellectual parents or of poor peasants who lead simple lives. All that the Golden Children have in common is awesome, unexplained mental powers.

In infancy, child prodigies usually display an astonishing command of language, literature, music or mathematics while children of a similar age are still struggling to speak their first words.

What we do not know is whether baby genius comes from inherited brain power, from a chance development in the womb, or an environmental factor at birth. One answer stems from an American experiment to try to produce Golden Children by genetic selection. The Nobel Sperm Bank in Escondido, California, was formed in 1980 by an elderly, eccentric millionaire, Robert Graham. It was to provide intelligent women who wanted to be mothers of superior babies with the male sperm of Nobel Prize-winning geniuses.

The aim of the sperm bank was, and still is, to increase dramatically the number of highly intelligent or gifted children in future generations. The first deliberately-conceived baby genius was born in 1982 to a 41-year-old unmarried psychologist, Afton Blake, in Los Angeles. She chose her baby's father from a portfolio, listing attributes which included good physical appearance and a high level of intelligence. The anonymous donor, identified by the sperm bank only as Number 28, is a brilliant computer scientist at a European university and an accomplished musician and athlete. His son, born in August 1982, was named Doron, an anagram of donor. By the time Doron was four months old, psychologists testing him at the University of California's Child Development Center declared that the baby had an IQ (Intelligence Quotient) of 200. The average rating is 100. At two years old, Doron was developing faster than children of the same age.

However, other child geniuses have astonished the world by their difference to their parents. One of the greatest geniuses and exceptional scientists of all time, Albert Einstein, was born the son of a bankrupt businessman in Ulm, West Germany, whose engineering workshop was barely profitable enough to support the family. The young Einstein spent much of his childhood visiting Bavarian taverns with his parents. His mother, although fond of music and literature, had no outstanding talents to pass on to her son.

By the time he was 14 years old, Albert Einstein had taught himself complex geometry and mathematics and was on his way to winning a place at the University of Zurich. In his mid-twenties he announced the first part of the Theory of Relativity and began to unlock the secrets of the Universe. Ten years later he had a scientific work published which explained the inner workings of the atom – and eventually led to the development of nuclear bombs and atomic power. Yet there had never been a hint of genius in the ordinary characteristics of his parents, Hermann and Pauline.

It was perhaps understandable that Wolfgang Amadeus Mozart, born in 1756, might show some musical ability. His father, Leopold, was himself a tolerable violinist. But the toddler outshone his father almost as soon as he could walk. At the age of three he taught himself to pick out chords on the keyboard of a harpsichord. At the age of five the child began to compose music while his father struggled to write down the score for him.

Soon Mozart mastered the technique of writing down musical notations for himself, and a year later performed before the Austrian Emperor in Vienna. At seven years old his first compositions were published. He gave recitals in Paris and Brussels, having taught himself to play the violin. The following year he played to George III in London, accompanied Queen Charlotte in an aria, wrote two symphonies and presented the score for one of his compositions to the British Museum.

His first opera, *La Finta Semplice,* was written at the age of 12. In the same year he wrote an operetta, two symphonies and a Mass. At 14 he was knighted by the Pope. Despite his dozens of symphonies and operas, Mozart finally died in poverty at the age of only 35, an enigmatic musical mystery and prodigy.

In the world of literature, the German poet and dramatist, Johann Goethe, and the British philosopher-economist, John Stuart Mill, were both able to read Greek by the age of three. Thomas Babington Macaulay, the 19th-century poet-historian, astonished and frightened his parents when, at only one year old, he looked out of the window of his nursery and asked profoundly, 'Is the smoke of that chimney coming from Hell?'

Conversely, the greatest playwright in the English language, William Shakespeare, was not a child prodigy. Nor was his genius passed on from his father, John. John Shakespeare was a prosperous businessman who overspent and in order to pay off his debts forced his son to leave school and seek

115

Ruth Lawrence received an Oxford University degree at 13.

employment. There is some evidence that Shakespeare was a teenage hooligan and thief, who was forced to flee from his home in Stratford after being caught deer poaching on the land of a local nobleman, Sir Thomas Lucy. Only in his late twenties did Shakespeare's timeless literary talent emerge and flourish.

In the 20th century, computer records have revealed a number of child prodigies in education. Wider access to university education has resulted in younger university entrants. The youngest entrant on record is Liu Xiaobin, the son of two teachers. Born in Hefei, China, in 1981, he passed his university exams at the age of five. At the age of two, Liu could read 3,600 complex Chinese characters.

Boy genius Andragone DeMello, born in 1977, became the youngest person to graduate from an American university when, at the age of 11, he gained a degree in mathematics from the University of California at Santa Cruz. Andragone first astounded his parents by saying 'Hello', when he was only seven weeks old. At two-and-a-half years old he was playing chess and working on geometry problems. At the age of three he calculated the volume of his bathwater and at four he was learning Greek, physics and philosophy. He was studying geology and geophysics at six years old and by the age of eight he had written complex computer programs.

His father, flamenco guitar player Augustine DeMello, admitted, 'I don't know where this amazing talent and genius comes from. He certainly hasn't inherited it from me. It sometimes frightens me being the parent of a child prodigy.'

In Britain, the youngest child prodigy to enter university is Ruth Lawrence. She gained a first class degree in mathematics at Oxford when she was only 13 and immediately began studying for a doctorate, hoping to beat the 18th-century record of Scottish prodigy Colin MacLaurin. (MacLaurin became Professor of Mathematics at Marischal College, Aberdeen, in 1717 when he was only 19 years old.)

From an early age, when she first showed signs of unusual intelligence, Ruth was coached intensively by her father: Harry Lawrence gave up his job as a computer consultant to become his daughter's full-time tutor. Many educational specialists who acknowledge Ruth's brilliant talent also claim that the relentless energy and instruction of her scientifically bright father has been a major factor in encouraging her success.

However, no one can account for the mysterious talents of baby Anthony McQuone of Weybridge, Surrey, who could speak Latin and quote Shakespeare at the age of two. His father, Anthony, claimed, 'I have no special talents and I have never had the ability to give Anthony any special coaching. He often corrects my grammar when I talk to him and he can produce such extraordinary facts from out of the blue that I have to buy an encyclopedia just to check what my baby son is telling me is correct.'

Anthony, who amuses himself by identifying and repeating the trademark symbols of 200 different models of motor car, has his own strange explanation for the source of his literary and linguistic knowledge. Interviewed by journalists in 1984, the two-year-old insisted that all the information was passed to him by a mysterious invisible friend, Adam. The toddler insisted that Adam was a grown-up with black hair, brown eyes, wearing a toga and *caliga* (latin for sandals). He added as an afterthought, 'Adam has a Van Dyke beard, too.'

Not only through intellectual achievement do child geniuses astonish the grown-up world. They can show the mature judgement and physical skill of experienced adults, or even beat them at their own games.

The youngest British international athlete was ten-year-old diver Beverly Williams, who competed against the USA in 1967. In 1988, 11-year-old Tom Gregory made sporting history by swimming the English Channel. The youngest ever boxing world title holder was Wilfred Benitz, who became light welter-weight champion in 1976 at 17 years old. The youngest international football player, Norman Whiteside, was the same age when he played for Northern Ireland in 1982. Five-year-old Coby Orr of Texas holds the record for the youngest golf player to score a hole in one, but the youngest to win the Open Golf Championship was 16-year-old Tom Morris, in 1868. Boris Becker was just a year older when he won the Men's Singles championship at Wimbledon in 1985, though Lottie Dod was only 15 when she won the Ladies Singles in 1887.

The mysterious world of child prodigies can bring wonder and delight to their parents, but it can also lead to misery and agony for little geniuses who feel alienated from children of their own age.

The brilliance of 12-year-old Ukrainian Seriozha Grishin gave him and his mother, Tamara, five years of bureaucratic torture from the Soviet education officials. He had been able to talk at the age of four months, walk at eight months and read and play the piano when he was little more than a year old.

The problems for Seriozha began when he was seven and his mother tried to enrol him in a local school in the town of Krivoy Rog, in the Ukraine. She wanted her gifted son to study along with children much older than him, but the school principal decided he would have to attend classes with other seven-year-olds. His teachers dismissed his talents, and his classmates called him an idiot, because his intellectual conversations were beyond them. They made him an outcast and used to lie in wait for him outside class to bully him and beat him up. His tormented mother, separated from her husband, eventually took him out of school and gave up her job as a music teacher to tutor him at home. The local authorities investigated the case, and committed Tamara Grishin to a mental hospital. They wrote on their official case file: 'Abnormal mother who does not work herself and refuses to let her son attend school. She is guilty of sheer disorder and failing to look after her child.'

Fortunately, within a few weeks friends and relatives had managed to get her released from the hospital. Then Tamara took her prodigious son to higher educational and medical specialists in Moscow and Kiev.

In 1987, the boy's genius was finally recognized when he was allowed to sit the entrance exam to the country's most prestigious seat of learning, Moscow State University, where he was promptly accepted into the Faculty of Physics with students ten years older than himself.

It is still a mystery whether babies can be developed into prodigies by ambitious parents who exploit their infant's abilities.

Perhaps Golden Children can simply be born to any parents, regardless of inherited intelligence.

Do child prodigies really have a mysterious gift that cannot be explained? Literary genius George Bernard Shaw was in no doubt about the futility of genetic selection as a way of producing child geniuses. The grizzled, bearded playwright was once approached by a gorgeous young actress who suggested that, with his brains and her beauty, they could produce a Golden Child to astound the world. He wrote to her, politely: 'But, alas, what if the child inherits MY looks and YOUR brains?'!

Hypnotism

Its critics decry it as one of the most dangerous of the Black Arts, its supporters praise it as a safe and sound way of unlocking the full potential of the human brain. The baffling mystery, which has caused centuries of impassioned argument between scientists, psychiatrists and psychologists, is the awesome power of hypnosis.

Is it a force for good or evil, or just a harmless delusion and an entertaining trick of stage performers? The scientific experts of the British Medical

Association have condemned stage hynotism as dangerous. Performers usually know little about the mental and emotional backgrounds of the volunteers whom they call upon, for the delight of their audiences, to perform bizarre tricks and actions under hypnosis. But other medical authorities claim that hypnotism, and especially self-hypnosis, is a powerful psychological tool which can help patients lead fuller, healthier and more confident lives.

Tales of altered human behaviour during trance-like rituals were common in the histories of priests of Ancient Greek temples and African witch doctors, but it was not until the 18th century that the possible power of hypnotic suggestion began to be studied in any depth by doctors and psychologists in modern Europe.

In the 1700s, Austrian doctor Franz Mesmer, a devoted astrologist, concluded that distant stars affected human behaviour through their weak sources of magnetism. If that was the case, he reasoned, then bringing his patients into actual contact with more powerful sources, by stroking magnets over their heads, should produce even more profound results.

He began to experiment with patients in his consulting rooms in Vienna, reporting that cases of hysteria, madness and nervous disorders were being cured after his patients had entered a semi-conscious dream state. Soon, Mesmer realized that he didn't even need to apply magnetic iron rods to his patients: simply by using his fingertips, lowering the lights in the room and talking soothingly to his subjects, he could produce the same results. This was not the power of magnetism, Mesmer decided, but some unexplained force flowing between him and his patient. He called it 'animal magnetism'.

The hundreds of patients who flocked to see Dr Mesmer soon coined a new definition − 'Mesmerism'. But the Viennese police who infiltrated the mysterious goings-on in his consulting rooms decided he was conducting spiritualist seances instead of medical sessions, and his practice was banned.

In 1770, Mesmer moved to Paris and his revolutionary techniques took the French capital by storm. By 1784, so many of his followers had begun the practice of Mesmerism that the French Academies of Sciences and Medicine began their own investigation at the request of King Louis XVI, who had become worried that the new techniques were swamping the study of conventional medical practice.

At the same time, Professor Chastenet de Puysegur, a former President of the Medical Society of Lyons, who was conducting his own experiments, observed a new phenomenon. Once he had his subjects in a trance, he could actually control their actions by the merest suggestion. He appeared to have total control over their own will. De Puysegur's conclusions, together with the Academy report, was enough to convince King Louis and his medical

Franz Anton Mesmer developed the doctrine of 'animal magnetism'.

authorities that Mesmerism was a dangerous cult of evil mind-benders who would corrupt and dominate French citizens.

Mesmer was discredited, and in 1789 he moved to Switzerland where he died in obscurity 36 years later, still convinced that he had tapped the power of the human mind, and embittered that he had been rejected by the leading researchers of orthodox medicine.

However, Mesmer's techniques lived on, not as a serious tool of medical research, but mostly as a form of public entertainment for stage shows and parlour games.

There was no further serious research until 1842, when hard-headed Scottish psychologist James Braid undertook his own experiments. Braid found he could induce a trance just by asking his patients to concentrate their vision on a bright light held before their eyes. The reactions of his patients he defined as 'somnambulism', literally sleep-walking, and he coined a new phrase for his work – hypnotism.

His work sparked off a revival of medical experiments, which included surgery being performed on willing patients who experienced no pain while doctors carried out major operations. However, most of the eminent surgeons of the day, like London specialist Sir Benjamin Brodie, who had watched a hypnotized patient having his leg amputated, dismissed the technique as little more than 'a debasing superstition'; and once again hypnotism became the entertaining tool of stage performers.

Even eminent medical men who still believed that hypnotism had some scientific value could not resist the temptation to demonstrate the demeaning qualities of their powers. There was, for instance, a celebrated 19th-century surgeon, Rudolf Heidenhain, who liked to conclude his lectures on hypnotism by putting some of his eminent colleagues in a trance and making them crawl on all fours on the floor, barking like dogs, or purring like cats and lapping up milk from imaginary saucers.

The Victorian obsession with hypnotism in the music halls of England further debased the technique. Audiences howled with laughter as willing volunteers clambered on stage and went through degrading acts like stripping off their clothes and trying to play music on imaginary instruments.

Later still, in the 20th century, even the sober and respectable directors of the BBC were humiliated and baffled when they decided to try to combine the entertainment value of a stage hypnotism act with a serious study of the phenomenon. It was in the early days of television, in 1946, when the BBC men conducted their own experiment. During a rehearsal in their broadcast studios at Alexandra Palace in north London, members of the production crew sat in a studio as a stage hypnotist put them in a trance. When the producer asked his cameramen and studio technicians to move to the next sequence in his script, he got no response: the entire production team at their camera viewfinders and in front of the monitor screens in the control room were all in a deep trance. The director eventually had to ask the hypnotist to free his staff from the mind-numbing effects of the trance and to snap them out of their frozen state.

After this event, the BBC decided they would never again attempt to broadcast any live display of hypnotism, for fear of sending the viewers of their fledgling broadcast service into hypnotic trances in front of their TV sets at home. And since then, the BBC have maintained a strict ban on broadcasting examples of hypnotists at work, although viewers are allowed to see subjects who are already in a trance, provided they cannot witness the actual act of hypnotism itself.

Six years later, in 1952, live demonstrations of hypnotism suffered another severe blow. A stage volunteer, Grace Rains-Bath, who had agreed to be hypnotised during a performance at a London theatre, sued hypnotist Ralph Slater who had 'regressed' her on stage until she behaved and acted like a young child. Mrs Rains-Bath claimed in court that she had suffered depression and anxiety and had cried like an infant for months afterwards. She was awarded damages against the stage performer.

Later that year, Parliament passed the Hypnosis Act, which gave local authorities the power to ban stage hypnotism shows. That ban throughout the whole of London remained in force until 1988.

Hypnosis has still been practised elsewhere with varying degrees of public acceptance or scepticism. One particular field where it has had a mixed reaction is in police work, where it has been used mainly to attempt to extract vital pieces of half-remembered evidence from victims and witnesses to crimes. In the United States, the Boston Police Department has a specialist Hypnosis Unit, which reports that in about 75 per cent of the cases in which they are asked to give assistance, enough new information has been provided by witnesses in a trance to give investigators new leads. Their senior investigator, Inspector Patrick Brady, explained: 'A person who has seen a violent crime committed or been the victim of a violent experience has an automatic tendency to blot that out of their mind. It is a fundamental self-protection mechanism to save that person from emotional trauma and psychological disturbance. Our job is to unblock that mental barrier through hypnosis and get our witness to recall details which their mind would sooner forget. We find that interviews under hypnosis are just as valuable in providing proof of innocence as proof of guilt.

'Someone falsely arrested and charged with committing a crime may come up with vital proof under hypnosis, perhaps remembering a key witness who will attest to his or her innocence. Hypnosis on a victim of a violent attack who wants only to forget their experience can help us construct an accurate identikit picture of their attacker. Other details which have been suppressed by the mind, like a car licence number, can also spill out of a subject in a trance and help us to solve vicious crimes.'

Although the evidence of hypnotised witnesses is often enough for police to pursue a fresh lead, it is only very rarely allowed to be presented in American courts. Sergeant Charles Diggett, a veteran New York cop who used investigative hypnosis in more than 400 cases during his career, added: 'Interviews under hypnosis must be videotaped and kept on file until the case is closed. In order for the tape to be accepted in court, the hypnotist has to be seen to be neutral throughout the session. They must keep silent whenever possible and let the witness do the talking. If an investigator prompts his subject or makes any suggestions, the information produced cannot be accepted as evidence.

'Even allowing for subconscious prompting, I firmly believe it is impossible for a hypnotist to manipulate his subject's mind. It is impossible to make someone say or do something against their will. Experiments have proved this time and time again. Hypnosis isn't mind control, it is only a trigger that can release what's already there by refreshing the memory.

'A person can tell lies under hypnosis, just as they might when giving a normal statement, or else, in rare cases, they can fantasize, but further investigation will eventually reveal the truth.'

But despite the American experience, in 1988 the British police forces were strongly advised against using hypnosis to obtain evidence. In a confidential notice to Britain's 43 police forces, Home Secretary Douglas Hurd warned that hypnotic evidence would be ruled as inadmissible in courts and that witnesses would not be cross-examined about anything they had recalled while in a trance.

Outside the fields of forensic and medical research, hypnosis has been hailed as a revived psychological tool by a new wave of practitioners. These people prefer to define their techniques as 'auto-suggestion', where their subjects are shown how to hypnotise themselves in order to increase positive aspects of their own personalities and mental powers.

Driving instructor Doug Beattie of Dundee was threatened with blacklisting by the Driving Instructors' Association after he revealed that he calmed his students' nerves by hypnotising them before their driving tests. He admitted: 'I make two visits to their homes in the two weeks before their test and hypnotise them. On the day of their test I take them to a side-street near the test centre and hypnotise them again to keep them calm, cool and collected during their driving exam. It seems to work. Eight out of ten pupils pass their test first time.'

Several leading celebrities also claim to have benefited from lessons in 'self-hypnosis'. Comedy actress and writer Lily Tomlin, who was struggling to complete a film script, claims she used self-hypnosis to speed up her writing and produce a box-office hit. Actor Sylvester Stallone used hypnosis to overcome shyness and lack of self-confidence – and to write the script of his enormously successful Rambo movies.

Nervous schoolchildren have been encouraged to pass exams, and sportsmen and women have equally been spurred on to greater achievements by hypnosis. Boxing champ Muhammad Ali, for example, used self-induced hypnosis as a 'psyching' process before his professional bouts.

Although London's Westminster Council lifted its 36-year ban on public performances of hypnotism in 1988, there were still adverse reports from around the world of innocent people suffering at the hands of stage hypnotists. In Italy, police had to scour Rome to trace stage hypnotist Giucas Casella after he had given a hypnosis demonstration on the national television network. Casella was found in a Rome hospital, recovering from a wound in his neck. He had inserted a metal skewer to demonstrate to his TV viewers that his mind could ignore pain while he was under a trance. The Rome police had gone in search of Casella after an urgent call from medical authorities in Palermo, where eight-year-old Giusto Durante had spent three hours in a trance after watching the television performance. The boy was unconscious, with his hands so tightly clasped together that his fingers had become swollen and black. Even powerful sedative drugs injected by doctors failed to relax his muscles. Young Giusto unclasped his blackened fingers only after the hypnotist shouted to him down the telephone: 'One, two, three, your hands are free!'

On another occasion, Scottish psychiatrist Dr Prem Misra warned that he was still giving treatment to 16 patients who had suffered after-effects from stage hypnosis performances. One was a man who still stripped off all his clothes every time he heard a hand-clap. Another was an elderly woman who had been 'regressed' to her youth, which had been spent in a Nazi death camp. She was now reliving the horrors anew, long after the mental scars had healed. A third was a young wife who had become schizophrenic after a stage hypnotist had convinced her, playfully, that her husband had been unfaithful to her.

Dr Misra explained: 'There are powerful mental forces at work in hypnotism which can be potentially very, very dangerous.'

Amnesia

Memory can be the fond recollection of a joyful past event, or the recapture of a painful moment which has caused grief and sadness. Whatever the emotion, the powers of recall hidden inside the human brain are a living record of our past experiences. Sometimes they can be recalled with startling clarity, at other times they are no more than a hazy recollection of fleeting moments in our own personal history.

Memory is also the function of our stored wisdom, a living record of our acquired learning, which gives us the ability and skill to tackle present-day tasks, from the performance of complex jobs to recognition of familiar, everyday objects, places and people.

But what happens deep inside the memory banks of the brain when a person is stricken by amnesia? Amnesia is not simply a period of forgetfulness. It is a profound mental helplessness which prevents victims from remembering any past events, trivial or crucial.

The memory cells, situated towards the rear of the brain, just above the portion which controls sight, are well protected inside the bony armour of the skull. Linked to other centres which command the mastery of thought, feeling, movement and recognition, the memory is capable of storing billions of bits of information in the form of electro-chemical signals. Neurological specialists have mapped the distinctly different areas of the brain accurately, but they are still unable to fully understand the unexplained mysteries of its inner workings.

Powers of mental storage and recall vary from individual to individual. Many so-called memory experts claim that memory resembles a muscle which can be strengthened and improved with constant exercise. Science knows of rare cases of 'eidetic' or 'photographic' memory – the ability to re-project remembered material just as if it is visually displayed and to be able to recall fine detail.

Photographic memory was the key factor in allowing a 28-year-old female bank clerk from Kenton, Middlesex, to give police an astonishingly accurate description of a man who broke into her flat and raped her. The attacker had assaulted her in the darkness of her bedroom, and had switched on a lamp for only a few seconds to steal some loose change from her purse. It was enough for the young woman to recall his features so precisely that the artist's impression she helped to draw for police was as accurate as a photograph. The rapist was arrested almost immediately and sentenced at the Old Bailey in 1986 to seven years imprisonment.

More usually, photographic memory is displayed as a curious mental oddity. The most prodigious memory man on record is Bhandanta Vicitsara, a Burmese monk who could recite from memory 16,000 pages of Bhuddist prayers. To give another example, engineer Dominic O'Brien of Guildford, Surrey, who suffered from dyslexia, was able to memorize the correct sequence of 312 playing cards displayed in front of him in a random sequence. Testers and umpires who shuffled six packs of cards spent 90 minutes showing him the cards, one at a time. One-and-a-half hours later, he was able to repeat the exact order of the cards, taking half an hour to recite them.

At the other end of the memory scale are the sufferers of amnesia who cannot recall key moments of their lives. Amnesia is usually the result of physical damage to the skull which actually injures the cells of the brain. Often, the brain recovers with only a gap in memory. Car crash victim Alan Woodward of Bristol, for example, spent a year in the twilight world of amnesia, unable to recognize his wife and two children, until his memory was jogged by a sports headline in a local newspaper. As soon as he saw it, he was able to reel off the 11 names of the players of his local football team. Afterwards the memory of his own personal life slowly began to return.

Another road accident victim, Nick Reading of Stockton, Warwickshire, had total amnesia at the age of 27 when he suffered head injuries. He could recall nothing of his childhood, his marriage or the birth of his first child. Even when he had recovered fully from the physical effects of his injuries, he remained unemployed, unable to remember the skills he had learned as an experienced and highly-paid bricklayer.

Physical injury is not the only cause of total amnesia. Traumatic terror can produce such a mental shock that a victim blots out the memory of it so effectively that they are unable to recall the event years later, regardless of how hard they try. One such event may have been the cause of the bout of amnesia that Hungarian-born Maria Tandi had, when she lost nearly all memory of the first 28 years of her life. By 1988, when she was 78, hospital officials in Claybury, Essex, where she had been a patient for half a century, had still not been able to piece together the origins of the severe fit of depression which had caused her loss of memory.

Maria, a former domestic servant in Wales, was first admitted to hospital when she lost the ability, or the will, to speak. Even 50 years later, she was still only able to mutter a few simple words and phrases. Maria was able to recall only fragments of her childhood. She remembered a garden with cherry trees and flowers in a remote corner of Eastern Hungary. Her next memory was of events nearly 20 years later, when she worked as a maid in an apartment in Dob-Utca, a smart residential district of Budapest. She could also recount the names of her six sisters, but could not describe them. Her mind remained blank, until she remembered a train journey across Europe and a short sea crossing to Dover, where she joined other refugee girls hoping to start a new life in England.

Shortly after Maria arrived in England, she received a letter from home, telling her of the death of her mother. Psychiatrists believe that the shock may have been so great that not only did Maria's memory close down, but she even forgot how to speak. Fifty years later, she was still living quite contentedly in her silent world, totally unaware of anything that had happened to her since 1938, including the cataclysm of World War II.

An equally tragic and mysterious case of amnesia struck BBC radio producer and medieval music historian Clive Wearing. In 1984, he suffered a brain inflammation when the virus, *Herpes simplex*, which normally causes blisters such as cold sores, suddenly flared up in his brain tissues. From then on, he lived in the terrifying world of a man locked into the present, with no memory of anything that had happened around him any longer than a few seconds before. He would often break down in tears and rush to his wife, Deborah, when he noticed her at the other end of the room (thinking he was having a long-awaited reunion with her) even though he had been talking to her only a few minutes before. The disastrous brain inflammation which almost cost the musician his life in a fevered coma that lasted for a month left him with irreversible amnesia.

It is a rare condition. Although about 50 people a year in Britain fall victim to the same illness, most of them make a full recovery. In an attempt to cope with the simple tasks of day-to-day living, Wearing kept a continuous diary of everything around him. His ability to read and write were unaffected, but he had difficulty reading his diary entries because, no matter how often he looked at the pages of the book, he could not remember his own handwriting. Within a minute of studiously poring over a diary entry, he would totally forget what he had read.

Mealtimes were a constant agony for him, as he frequently ate until he was sick, thinking he had only just sat down to dinner and forgetting that he had already been at the table for half-an-hour and consumed several courses. He was aware only of the food which was then in front of him, and did not realize he had eaten his fill.

Surprisingly, his awareness only of a small segment of the present did not rob him of his musical talents. As part of a documentary research film, Clive Wearing was taken back to Cambridge University, where he had first graduated with a degree in music, and was asked to play the organ in King's

College. It was an experience he had enjoyed countless times before as a student and a graduate, but when he saw the chapel organ he told the film crew and his wife: 'I've never seen this before. What am I supposed to do?'

However, once seated on the organ stool, Wearing played the instrument perfectly, to his own amazement. Seconds after he completed the organ recital, he turned round. Seeing his wife, he grasped her emotionally, not remembering that she had sat behind him during the entire performance. Turning round again, he saw the organ and was convinced, yet again, that he was seeing it for the first time. Then he asked to be introduced to the members of the documentary film crew, who had been his constant companions for days.

Later, when Wearing saw the film footage of his performance at the college organ, he watched in bewilderment, not able to remember the occasion and hardly daring to believe that he was witnessing himself playing the music. By the time he had finished watching the film, he could not even remember the opening sequence of the documentary or the scene where he had played the King's College organ.

For the largest group of amnesia sufferers – elderly people striken by senile dementia – there is some hope on the horizon. More than half a million people in Britain are victims of the brain disorder Alzheimer's disease, which relentlessly robs them of their memory and their chance of a fulfilling, independent life. Researchers and scientists have now discovered synthetic hormones which can alter the workings of the human mind.

One of Britain's most distinguished scientists, Nobel Prize winner Professor Archer Martin, had to abandon his pioneering studies in 1984 when, at the age of 74, he contracted Alzheimer's disease and began to lose his memory. Although the disease was in a relatively early stage, Professor Martin found he could no longer remember the details of notes he had just studied, and specialist doctors at Addenbrooke's Hospital, in Cambridge, warned him that nothing could be done to halt the decline of his brilliant mind. Within a few years, they told him, he would be 'a human vegetable'.

By 1988, after Professor Martin had volunteered to become a guinea pig in trials of a new experimental memory drug THA at London's Institute of Psychiatry, his astonishing mental powers began to show dramatic signs of recovery. As he prepared to renew his own research career he found that, for the first time in years, he was able to analyse and remember complicated articles in the science journal *Nature*. He said: 'My own life had begun to fall apart around me. I even missed presentations and awards ceremonies because, after I set out to attend them, I would forget where I was going and I would board the wrong train or plane. Now my brain has been restored to useful work, I can enjoy reading research papers once more, although I had to renew my subscriptions to scientific journals. I had completely forgotten that my wife had cancelled them because they were useless to me when I had no real memory to benefit from them.'

Even though researchers still do not understand the workings of the human memory or the emotions milling around inside our highly developed brains, they expect the 1990s will produce a spectacular breakthrough in 'brain pills' that may make amnesia only a memory. Moreover, scientists predict a new range of synthetic hormones that will totally alter human mental abilities and emotions. At Utrecht in Holland, university research Professor David De Wied prophesied that the discovery of a new 'memory drug', the hormone DGAVP, will wipe out the scourge of amnesia and may even be used on healthy patients to dramatically increase their memory power. Also in Utrecht, the 'contentment pill', based on the hormone ACTH 4–9, has been shown to produce feelings of wellbeing and confidence in depressed elderly people who have almost given up the will to live. This drug has also been found to increase concentration and motivation in healthy young people.

In Canada the 'forget drug', the hormone oxytocin, which is released naturally in women to ease them through the pain of childbirth, has been tested on disturbed psychiatric patients to wipe out the memories of traumatically disturbing experiences that have left victims deeply emotionally scarred. Dr De Wied predicts confidently; 'We will be able in the future to affect all the processes of the brain. And if, as it seems likely, the ageing process of the brain is caused by the deficiency of hormones, we will be able to replace them and perhaps even reverse the ageing process itself.'

Out-of-Body Experiences

I t is an accepted scientific fact that no two bodies can occupy the same space at the same time. But there is one mystery which has puzzled philosophers and researchers for centuries: Can one body occupy two distant spaces at the same time? Or, is it possible to be in two different locations in the same instant?

Many recent studies of 'out-of-body experiences' claim that it is perfectly possible for a person's own psyche to drift out of their body and move to another location, while their physical being stays in its original position, undisturbed.

Some personal testimonies to such experiences, or 'astral projections', as they are defined by mystics and psychics, may just be the result of delusions and imagination. Most of the first-hand accounts come from patients who have undergone surgery. Usually, their experiences can be accounted for by the anaesthetics they have been administered, which have been known to produce wild fluctuations of brain behaviour in unconscious patients. But other, more positively credible reports, have been compiled by research into hospital patients who have actually been declared clinically dead and who have been resuscitated after a period of time – sometimes many minutes. Having returned to consciousness, they have given similar accounts of experiencing their souls parting from their bodies and travelling in an unknown dimension.

In many primitive cultures, the belief that the soul can leave the body and travel to another place runs deep. Ancient Indian religious teachings detail how supernatural powers can be achieved through meditation, including the ability to leave the physical body and fly through the sky. Even more recent folklore says it is unwise to wake a sleepwalker, because it may prevent the soul being able to re-enter the body, which is in a physical, but soulless, state.

Independent eye-witness evidence of a person being physically, or spiritually, in two places at the same time is virtually unknown; but the evidence seems to exist in the case of the Catholic friar St Anthony of Padua. St Anthony lived from 1195 to 1231 and travelled as a preacher in northern Italy and southern and central France. He was an honoured visitor to many churches and was in great demand as a guest preacher throughout his far-flung parish. According to meticulous medieval church records, he preached two memorable sermons – in two different places at the same time.

While preaching a sermon in a church in Limoges in France in 1226, during which all the congregation watched their guest friar with careful attention, St Anthony very abruptly stopped in the middle of his prayers. He pulled the cowl of his robes over his head and knelt silently for several minutes. The congregation waited, restlessly, until the preacher finally rose to his feet again and continued his address to the churchgoers. Only later that day did the townsfolk of Limoges realize that the Saint's brief interruption to his devotions was not an opportunity for solitary meditation. To their amazement and delight they found that while the figure of the friar had been kneeling in full sight of the entire congregation, he had appeared at the same time before the congregation of another church several kilometres away and read the lesson during the service. Then he had disappeared from the pulpit just as mysteriously as he had arrived.

Although St Anthony himself never left any written record of his apparent out-of-body experiences, the same phenomenon has been described many times by figures as diverse as eminent scientists and tortured prisoners. Dr Auckland Geddes, later Lord Geddes, described his own experiences in clinical detail in a paper presented to the Royal Medical Society of Edinburgh in 1937. Lord Geddes recounted to his fellow members of the respected Society how he had been in bed at home, stricken with acute food poisoning, when he suddenly became gravely ill. 'I wanted to ring for assistance, but found I could not, so I gave up the attempt,' he said.

'I realised I was very ill but at no time did my consciousness appear to be dimmed, but I suddenly realized that my consciousness was separating from another consciousness which was also "me".

'Gradually, I realized that I could see not only my body and the bed in which it was, but everything in the whole house and garden, and then I realized that I was seeing not only things at home, but in London as well, in fact wherever my attention was directed. I was free in a time dimension of space.'

Geddes recalled how his spirit re-entered his body, in terms amazingly similar to the accounts of others who have experienced the same detached feelings of hovering between life and death. He told the meeting that he saw his maid enter his bedroom. 'I realized she got a terrible shock,' he said. 'I saw her hurry to the telephone. I saw my doctor leave his own patients at his surgery and hurry over to my house and I heard him say, "He is nearly gone." I heard him quite clearly speaking to me on the bed, but I was not in touch with my own body and I could not answer him.

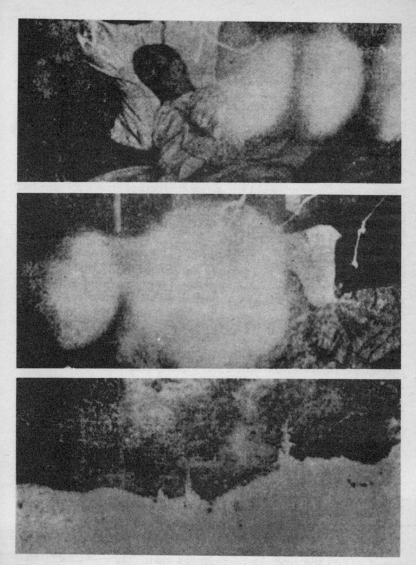

These photographs show the spirit leaving a patient's body.

'I was really cross when he took a syringe and rapidly injected my body. As my heart began to beat more strongly, I was drawn back and I was intensely annoyed because I was so interested and I was just beginning to understand where I was and what I was seeing.

'I came back into my body, really angry at being pulled back, and once back, all the clarity of vision of everything and anything disappeared and I was just possessed of a glimmer of consciousness which was suffused with pain.

'I think the whole thing simply means that, but for medical treatment, I was dead to the three dimensional world.'

The experience of being able to roam freely through space and time is consistent with the account of a violent prisoner, Ed Morrell, who was held in Arizona State Penitentiary in 1910. While in prison, Morrell frequently had to be restrained by warders and put into a straitjacket. Morrell claimed that his torture was added to when the bindings were soaked in water and slowly shrunk, squeezing him so tightly that he lapsed into unconsciousness. During these agonized blackouts, he felt his spirit float free and he was able to travel at will, even examining the perimeter area around the prison in accurate detail, in readiness for an escape plan. Morrell also claimed that he could direct his spirit freely across the United States and that in one of his out-of-body travels he met the woman he was later to track down and marry after his release from the penitentiary.

Morrell told the story of his experiences later in San Francisco to writer Jack London, who used them as the basis for his book *The Star Rover*.

A large amount of detailed research into out-of-body experiences was gathered by American psychiatrist Dr Elisabeth Khubler-Ross, who spent over 20 years counselling terminally ill patients, young and old. Khubler-Ross's records of the graphic accounts she received from her patients hovering on the brink of death tally almost exactly with the reported experiences of Lord Geddes made some 40 years before.

The patients told the psychiatrist about their sensations of floating free, feeling at peace and spiritually powerful, before being summoned back, usually reluctantly, to their pain-racked bodies. She documented her findings in her book *On Death and Dying*, published in 1970, and added her own personal endorsement later: 'Before I started working with dying patients, I did not believe in life after death. I now believe in it beyond a shadow of a doubt.'

Dr Khubler-Ross reported that many of her patients who had come to accept the inevitable outcome of their terminal diseases were convinced that their spirits left their bodies for prolonged periods, during which they were surrounded with a powerful, peaceful force, and that they often encountered dead friends and relatives who had come to prepare them for a new existence after death. The patients felt great joy and happiness, and few of them felt any desire to return to their physical bodies. Many of them who had suffered short periods of clinical death with no detectable heartbeat or pulse were drawn back to their bodies only out of a sense of responsibility to those they would leave behind, or by the reassurance of a vision of a heavenly presence who explained that it was not yet time for them to die. Dr Khubler-Ross was convinced that many of her patients who had floated free of their bodies before being medically revived had no fear of finally dying.

The writer, novelist and war correspondent Ernest Hemingway had his own visions of death when he was wounded by a burst of shrapnel while acting as a volunteer ambulanceman in Italy during World War I. He did not exactly undergo any great spiritual surges as he lay seriously injured and semi-conscious, waiting for the battlefield first aid which saved his life. In his own terse style, Hemingway reported it as: '. . . my soul, or something, coming right out of my body, like you'd pull a silk handkerchief out of a pocket by one corner. It flew around and then came back and went in again, and I wasn't dead any more.'.

Hemingway, who, in 1961, in a fit of depression, committed suicide by shooting himself, never explained if the experience gave him any confidence, or doubts, in the prospect of life after death.

Out-of-body experiences are not solely confined to seriously ill patients, or those under sedation or close to death. American researcher Dr Charles Tart, of the University of California, undertook a series of experiments to see if healthy volunteers who claimed they underwent frequent out-of-body experiences could produce any evidence under carefully controlled laboratory conditions. He put his volunteers on a bed in a darkened room, with electrical contacts wired to their head to record their brain wave patterns. Also in the room, hidden on a shelf out of sight of the volunteer, was a slip of paper with a number written on it. If the volunteer attempted to get up out of bed to try to cheat, by clambering up high to read the hidden number, the electrical contacts would break and the deception would be detected immediately. As an added precaution to prevent cheating by collusion with any of his own staff, Dr Tart used a random number generator to compute the figure 25132, which he wrote on the slip of paper himself without anyone else knowing the chosen number.

Dr Tart's most convincing volunteer was a young woman who claimed that she had enjoyed out-of-body experiences since her childhood and could induce them almost any time she wished. On her first night in the experimental 'bedroom' nothing out of the ordinary happened and the electrical brainwave patterns showed that she had a normal night's sleep. On the second night, she claimed she had floated free of her body and she had seen a clock on the wall, even though the clock was hidden from her view as she lay on the bed. She reported that she had seen the clock clearly and read the time on it as 3.15 a.m. The printout of her brainwave patterns was checked against a time recorder and the researchers discovered that her sleep had become erratic and disturbed at exactly that time.

On the third night, the volunteer again reported a vision of the hidden clock in the early hours of the morning, and the time of her experience coincided exactly with the same brainwave disturbances shown on the recorder. On the fourth night, concentrating deeply before she retired to bed, the volunteer awoke in the morning to repeat, with complete accuracy, the digits on the slip of paper lying on the shelf above her. She also said she had glanced at the clock as she read the number, and gave the time at around 6.00 a.m. The researchers later confirmed that her sleeping brainwave patterns had jumped wildly at 5.57 a.m., around the time she described her spirit as floating free of her body.

But do these crude experiments, or the personal recollections of eminent doctors, writers and hospital patients, really prove that men and women can travel away from their bodies and project their spiritual beings to other places on earth and into different dimensions? Since the publication of Dr Khubler-Ross's research, thousands of people have come forward to testify to similar experiences. Could all these just be delusions and illusions, nightmares and fits of troubled sleep?

The respected, pragmatic scientist Dr Carl Sagan of NASA's space experimental programme has his own theory, which would mean that almost anyone is capable of such an experience, and would regard it as a vivid, genuine memory of a truly spiritual event. He explains: 'Every human being has already had an experience like that of travellers who return from the land of death; the sensation of flight and emergence from darkness into light; an experience in which the heroic figure may be dimly perceived, bathed in radiance and glory. There is only one comon experience that matches this description.

'It is called birth.'

Chapter Five

BEYOND THE REALMS OF SCIENCE

Can we really believe that the powers of high-technology have reached such sophistication that we are on the brink of being able to make radio contact with aliens in outer space? You may laugh, but a number of extremely eminent scientists think we can. However, no matter how we marvel at 20th-century scientists and inventors for their brilliance, foresight and ingenuity, it seems that primitive civilizations, such as the Nazca Indians or the Dogon tribesmen, or the ancient practitioners of acupuncture could have told them more than a thing or two ...

Alien Contact

Ever since primitive man first drew himself upright and stared up at the heavens, he has pondered the eternal question: Is there life out there? For thousands of years we have been enthralled by the awesome prospect of creatures, or beings, existing out there in other galaxies, living in civilizations far more technologically advanced than our own. The terrible bug-eyed monsters of science fiction may only have been the product of writers' imaginations, but to millions of readers such creatures are real glimpses into the future.

In our galaxy alone, there are more than 100,000 million stars, and according to eminent astronomer Professor Archibald Roy, of Glasgow University, at least one-fifth are stable and cool, like our own Sun. About half of those, some 10,000 million stars, also have planets – the most important single requirement for developing life. Astronomers hope that many of these planets will be surrounded by organic 'fog' containing vital DNA-like molecules which could be the key to life itself.

In the late 50s, the Chinese-born astrophysicist Su-Shu Huang of North-western University, Illinois, described the types of conditions in which life could exist beyond our galaxy. It should be neither too hot, so that water would evaporate, nor too cold, so that it would be permanently frozen. With a combination like this, there is no logical reason why extraterrestrial life should not take root and flourish.

The dream of sending or receiving messages from aliens in outer space is as old as man himself. Before the discovery of radio waves, we had few reliable means of sending messages over even short distances. In ancient civilizations, beacons of burning wood on hilltops were a simple, effective signalling system; but these could only spell out the most simple of messages, usually a sign of alarm. The invention of the electric telegraph by Samuel Morse in 1836 was, therefore, a great scientific leap forward. With a distinct code of short or long bursts of electricity, the whole alphabet could be used to send elaborate and clearly understood messages.

Morse Code was not restricted only to pulses transmitted down a telegraph wire. The code could work equally well by using flashes of light beamed out by a lantern, or by rays of sunlight reflected off a mirror. It was this that gave the French inventor Charles Cros the idea of constructing a giant mirror. He would use it to flash bursts of reflected sunlight from Earth to Mars, in the hope of making contact with Martians. The mirror would be tilted back and forth in a such a way that beams of light could be flashed on and off.

There were, however, problems with Cros's idea. A mirror large enough to be able to send light as far as outer space would have to be so big, it would have been impossible to tilt it. Also, there was no guarantee that the Martians, if indeed there were any, would recognize it as a message at all: it might be just light reflecting off a giant terrestrial lake. Besides, how would they recognize a message in Morse Code if they saw one? And how would they signal back to Earth? Needless to say, when Cros died in Paris in 1888, the idea died with him.

Later, engineers working for the American inventor Thomas Edison came up with a more practical idea. They proposed building a giant floating raft on Lake Michigan, USA, with arms ten miles long, strung with the newly patented electric light bulbs Edison had invented. These would be switched on for ten minutes, then off for ten minutes, giving a clear indication to any watchers in space that an intelligent civilization on Earth was trying to make contact. However, inventive and curious though he was, Thomas Edison was also a hard-headed businessman. He decided that the tens of thousands of light bulbs needed for the experiment would be better used for the more down-to-earth purposes of illuminating the homes and streets of New York and swelling his fortune, as well as for providing finance for more mundane experiments he had in mind. So this idea did not get far, either.

In the 19th century, the thought of contact with alien life sent a thrill of expectation through many curious minds, and feelings of horror in others. In 1898, the science fiction writer H G Wells gripped their imagination with his sci-fi horror story, *War of the Worlds*, in which Earth is invaded by Martians in deadly war machines. But any real attempts to contact other planets were viewed by many Victorians as an invitation to trouble: civilizations in outer space might see Earth as an easy target and come down to invade it.

Nevertheless, one Paris newspaper publisher of the time was bold enough to offer a prize of 100,000 francs for anyone who could make contact with alien life in our own galaxy, or even further out in space. As a concession to thousands of fearful readers, who warned him not to encourage their fellow countrymen to dabble in the unknown, he made one exception to the rules of the competition: there would be no prize for anyone raising an answer from Mars. The publisher explained that since everyone was pretty certain there was probably intelligent life on Mars anyway, communicating with Martians would be too easy, and it wasn't worth him risking his money! In the event, no one claimed the prize, and many Europeans, still badly rattled by the graphic fiction of H G Wells, heaved a sigh of relief that reckless scientists weren't going to advertise their presence to potentially hostile aliens after all.

But whether we like it or not, we on Earth have been beaming signals into outer space since we began radio broadcasting during the early decades of this century. Radio and television programmes broadcast around the world 'leak' out into space, and although their signals grow weaker and weaker over the vast distances, it is possible they may be intercepted in some remote galaxy.

Many scientists have already tried to unscramble incoming radio signals from the endless crackle of natural cosmic radio waves that swamp the universe. But which radio frequency they should choose to listen into, or which ones they should transmit their own messages from, is anybody's guess. Here on Earth, our radio stations all select their own individual frequencies and wavelengths to avoid their signals interfering with each other; so the job of sorting out the millions of radio frequencies and identifying alien broadcasters seems an almost impossible task.

In 1943, Dutch astronomer Hendrick Christoffel van den Hulst came up with the most logical answer so far in identifying frequencies from outer space. He calculated that if hydrogen atoms changed their energy state through cosmic influences, they would emit a tiny burst of radio energy in the 21-centimetre radio wavelength. Since hydrogen is the most abundant element in the universe, any advanced civilization with a knowledge of atomic physics and radio waves would almost certainly have discovered it. Thus, broadcasting and receiving on the 21-centimetre waveband would provide a common, intergalactic radio network.

The first official, methodically planned attempt at contacting alien life via radio waves was made in 1960, when American radio astronomer Dr Frank Drake turned the 85-foot-diameter dish antenna of the National Radio Observatory at Green Bank, West Virginia, towards the stars Tau Ceti and Epsilon Eridani. He was particularly interested in these two stars, because they appear to be of the same breed as our own Sun, and also because, on the cosmic scale, both are relatively close to us, just 11 light years away. (A light year is the distance light, and a radio signal, travels in one year, about six million, million miles.) Within 12 light years of our home planet there are 18 star systems with 26 stars and probably hundreds of unseen planets. Dr Drake's experimental radio probe, therefore, pointed at a potentially fertile part of the galaxy. The experiment was codenamed Project OZMA, after Frank L Baum's mythical Land of Oz. The project was conducted in strict secrecy, because the scientists involved feared public ridicule or criticism for wasting valuable research time and equipment. Dr Drake listened cont-inuously, and unsuccessfully, for three months before admitting that intelli-gent life so close to Earth would really be too much to hope for. 'It would be a case of celestial overpopulation,' he told colleagues.

Just in case there is a possibility that alien civilizations have evolved, but have no knowledge of radio waves, Dr Drake has employed another method of letting the rest of the universe know that there is intelligent life on Earth. One of the leading scientific advisers on the 1972 Pioneer probe project, he was involved in developing the cosmic 'message in a bottle', which was thrown out into the oceans of space. The space probe, designed to explore the far-flung planet Jupiter, was launched on a special path to let it spin into deep space after it had completed its survey mission. Attached to the side of the spacecraft is a plaque, engraved with a coded message, showing the location of the planet Earth and a diagram of a woman and a man raising his hand in a greeting. Also included is a plain hint for the finder to try calling Earth on the 21-centimetre radio wavelength.

In 1976, four years after the Pioneer project began, the radio search for messages from outer space resumed again. By this time it was thought there was a slim chance that a patrolling alien spacecraft might have spotted and captured the drifting Pioneer probe as it continued its endless journey through space. American astronomers Benjamin Zuckerman and Patrick Palmer, also at Green Bank Observatory, tuned into the radio wavelength shown on the Pioneer probe. For four long years their research staff took it in turns to listen in for broadcasts, but they heard nothing but silence. Pioneer is probably still lost in the wandering debris of space, and it looks as though no one out there has yet read its message.

According to scientific author Ian Ridpath, it is just as well; for Ridpath believes the figure of a man with an upraised arm may be considered a threatening character by alien life forms. He experimented using the same gesture towards a cageful of rhesus monkeys, who form part of the same evolutionary scale as man. The monkeys thought he was about to attack, and they launched themselves towards the bars of their cage in angry defiance.

A far more colourful and welcoming message was blasted off into space in 1977. This was aboard the twin Voyager space capsules that flew to the planet Mars, the fictional home of the threatening aliens in *War of the Worlds*. The spacecraft carries two video discs that electronically portray life on 20th-century Earth. The sounds of nature are represented by the songs of birds and other animals, and peaceful greetings from the varied races and peoples on Earth are recorded in 55 different languages. Scientists admit that the chances of the Pioneer or Voyager probes being detected and recovered by alien life forms are so remote as to be beyond calculation. Travelling at only a few thousand miles a minute, the spacecraft will take hundreds of years to leave our own planetary system and reach distant galaxies.

The main hopes of opening a line of communication between us and the stars still lie in radio waves, travelling at the speed of light, and most research efforts are being concentrated in that direction.

Although Project OZMA lapsed, it was not forgotten, and it became the forerunner of dozens of schemes for eavesdropping on space. For instance, in America there is an organization called the Search for Extraterrestrial Intelligence. Known as SETI, it is backed by agencies like NASA. Film director Steven Spielberg, who made millions of dollars out of his science fiction hit film *E.T.*, is one of the many sponsors who has provided funding for their Project META, an 84-foot radio telescope hunting for unusual microwave frequencies in 'hot' areas of space. The sensitive piece of listening equipment is tucked away in the apple and peach orchards of Harvard University in Massachusetts, and the project was devised by scientist, writer and broadcaster Carl Sagan. SETI is now planning a major seven-year search, scheduled to begin on Columbus Day, 12 October 1992. This will be a coordinated world-wide effort, using newly-developed equipment capable of monitoring up to 70,000 radio channels. With the addition of new computer technology, it should soon be able to listen in on 10 million frequencies. Another phase of the project will include beaming messages to every single one of the detectable stars in the universe, in the hopes of getting a reply.

So, the race is well and truly on to find out if there is anyone out there; but it will be a long one. Even at the speed of light, a radio message may take 20 or 30 years to reach the nearest alien civilization. And it will take equally long for any aliens to send a reply back to Earth. The whole process will be rather like a very expensive, interplanetary telephone conversation, where the callers on each end of the line can only exchange brief phrases every few decades!

In the meantime, the babble of radio and television waves that have erupted from Earth since the turn of the century have a long headstart on the more recent messages of encouragement sent out by the dedicated scientists. If an alien civilization could actually decode and understand those early broadcasts, they could have already listened to radio reports of world wars, famines and disasters, and seen television broadcasts of soap operas, game shows and Presidential elections.

They may have decided that, judging by what they have heard and seen so far, they just don't want to return our calls.

The Dogon

For the 2 million members of the primitive Dogon tribe, scratching out an existence in the African republic of Mali on the edge of the Sahara Desert, life has changed little over the centuries. The tribespeople live in scattered villages, in dwellings made of mud and straw. They tend their flocks of scrawny goats, plant and reap meagre harvests of grain, and gather firewood on the sparse cliffs of the Bandiagara Plateau, 300 miles south of Timbuktu, where their ancestors settled some 500 years ago. And they worship their gods in the sky, lavishing particular reverence on the brilliant twinkling lights of the star system of Sirius, the brightest star in the night sky.

Many other tribes pay homage to the bright beacon of Sirius, beaming across space from 8.7 light years away, one of the closest stars to Earth. It is quite understandable that the attention of the early civilizations of the Northern hemisphere should be attracted to Sirius, because of its overwhelming prominence over all the other stars. The ancient Egyptians based their annual calendar on the rising of Sirius at certain times of the year, which they knew heralded the annual flooding of the Nile River.

But the belief and faith of the Dogon tribe is unique. For five centuries they have worshipped not just the vivid light of Sirius, but also its white dwarf companion star, Sirius B, invisible to the naked eye. What is so amazing is that the ancestors of the Dogon tribe had known, with certainty, of the position of Sirius B without the use of any powerful telescopes or precise astronomical instruments.

It was not until the middle of the 19th century that astronomers in Europe and America began to suspect the existence of another star close to Sirius. Laborious detailed observations and calculations of the irregularities of its orbit led them to conclude that the gravitational force of its hidden companion was exerting enormous force on Sirius. Then, in 1862, while testing a new telescope, American astronomer Alvan Graham Clark caught the first glimpse of the dense white dwarf companion. He named it Sirius B.

It was not until 60 years later that English scientist Sir Arthur Eddington first explained why the tiny Sirius B could cause such wild wobbling in the orbit of its much bigger adjacent star. He published his findings in 1928, explaining for the first time how Sirius B was a white dwarf, a giant star, which had collapsed under the power of its own mass to a fraction of its original size, but still exerted a powerful gravitational pull on neighbouring star Sirius.

Eventually in 1970, after the advent of the space age, sophisticated telescope lenses and highly sensitive cameras finally captured the first images of Sirius B. It was a major triumph for the precise calculations of the modern scientific astronomers.

To the Dogon tribe, however, all this was old news. It only confirmed what they had known all along. They had known for centuries that Sirius B was out there in space. They even had their own name for it – Po Tolo. They knew it was composed of super-dense cosmic material and they knew it orbited round Sirius in an elliptical path every 50 years.

They knew all this and they had known it from the beginning of their unwritten history, they explained. And they knew it because they were originally taught the secrets of the stars and planets and given the basic elements of their civilization by alien visitors from the Sirius star system!

How could these African tribespeople have discovered the precise scientific secrets of distant galaxies and planets so far ahead of sophisticated scientists armed with the benefits of modern technology? Their explanation of visitors from outer space is patently absurd and incredible. But the only alternative answer is just as unbelievable.

In 1931, two of France's most eminent anthropologists, Marcel Griaule and Germaine Dieterlen, arrived on the Bandiagara Plateau to make a study of the Dogon tribe. They had decided to devote several years of extended research into the origins and culture of the tribe. Drawn deeper and deeper into Dogon civilization, they virtually lived with the tribe for the next 21 years.

When Griaule and Dieterlen arrived, they found a tribe already steeped in the knowledge of the secrets of Sirius. Their religious rituals revolved around homage to Sirius, its hidden companion Sirius B, and a third, as yet undiscovered star. The symbols of the star system were woven into the patterns of their blankets, in designs which seemed to be hundreds of years old. They were depicted on their pottery, their wooden carvings and on the clay walls of their shrines.

Sir Arthur Eddington's discovery of Sirius B in 1928 was only known to a handful of astronomical students in England. The arrival of the two anthropologists on the Bandiagara Plateau was only three years later. Is it possible that in that brief space of time an entire semi-literate population could have pirated Sir Arthur's scholarly work and incorporated it into a fake tribal history, complete with fraudulent artefacts of cloth and pottery, just to impress and fool two French researchers?

It's doubtful that the anthropologists knew enough about recent astronomical discoveries to be much impressed by such an elaborate confidence trick. It took 15 years before Marcel Griaule was trusted sufficiently by the elders of the tribe. Then, he was indoctrinated into their occult ceremonies and was initiated into the creed of the alien visitor from Sirius, whom the Dogon called 'The Nommo'. According to the elders, the Nommo was a weird, amphibious creature from space, who had come to spread civilization on Earth and who had given the Dogon the beginnings of their unique culture.

After 20 years' experience of the history of the Dogon, the anthropologists published their historic research in the prestigious *Journal of the Society of African Research*. The paper, entitled *A Sudanese Sirius System,* explained in great detail the Dogon's mysterious advanced knowledge of planetary and stellar systems. It concluded, with cautious understatement: 'The problem of knowing how, with no instruments at their disposal, men could know of the movements and certain characteristics of virtually invisible stars has not been settled.'

For Marcel Griaule it was the culmination of his life's work. When he died in 1956, a quarter of a million Dogon tribespeople gathered at his funeral in Mali to pay their respects.

Griaule's long-time partner in research, Germaine Dieterlen, left Africa and returned to Paris to take up the post of Secretary General of the Society for African Studies at the Museum of Mankind. It was there that the additional joint research she published in 1965 for the French National Institute of Ethnology caught the imagination of American scholar Robert Temple. Temple, an authority on Sanskrit and Oriental studies, travelled to Paris for lengthy interviews with Dieterlen and journeyed to Mali, determined to get to the bottom of the mystery of the Dogon's mythology about visitors from outer space. Afterwards, he admitted: 'In the beginning I was just investigating. I was sceptical. I was looking for hoaxes, thinking it couldn't be true. But then I began to discover more and more pieces which fitted.'

The primitive tribespeople patiently explained to Temple how The Nommo, whom they described as 'the monitor of the Universe, guardian of its spiritual principles, dispenser of rain and master of water', had landed in a spaceship 'ark' in the north-east of their country early in the tribe's history.

Temple reported in his 1976 book, *The Sirius Mystery*: 'The Dogon describe the sound of the landing of the ark. They say the word of Nommo was cast down by Him in the four directions as He descended, and it sounded like the echoing of four large stone blocks being struck with stones by children according to special rhythms in a very small cave.

Presumably a thunderous vibrating sound is what the Dogon are trying to convey. One can imagine standing in a cave and holding one's ears at the noise. The descent of the ark must have sounded like a jet aircraft landing on a runway at close range.'

Dogon priests described how the ark from Sirius raised a whirlwind of dust as it finally settled on the dry dusty earth. Then, they told Temple what they knew about the solar system, how the surface of the Moon was 'dry and dead like dry, dead blood'. In crude drawings in the sand they retraced ancient outlines showing Saturn with a ring around it, the movements of the planets around the Sun, the spinning of the Earth on its axis and the orbit of Venus. They scratched out a sand drawing of the planet Jupiter showing the four major moons circling round it, and they claimed the diagram dated back centuries before Galileo had first seen those moons on his telescope.

To demonstrate their knowledge of the close-packed material of Sirius B, the compacted white dwarf, a Dogon priest produced a single grain of their cereal crop. The stellar matter of Po Tolo, he explained, was so dense that even a grain was so massive 'that all earthly beings combined cannot lift it'. It was a stunningly accurate description of the mass of a dwarf star, and one that could hardly be bettered by any precise scientific definition.

The priest also described a second, unseen red dwarf star orbiting Sirius. This star, he said, was not as dense as Sirius B, or Po Tolo, but was four times lighter in mass. The Nommo visitor came from a planet which circled this undiscovered star.

For Temple and other researchers, the mystery of the advanced astrological knowledge of the Dogon is still unsolved. It is possible that members of the tribe learned basic astronomical sciences from colonial French academies which had been established in their area as recently as the beginning of the 20th century, or even from the Moslem University which flourished in the provincial capital of Timbuktu in the 16th century. Further back in history it seems certain that the Dogon tribe, who originated from the northern coast of Africa, along the shores of Algeria, Libya and Egypt, might well have been in contact with advanced Mediterranean cultures.

Indeed, Mediterranean myth is rich in legends of strange amphibious creatures. Such legends brought a civilizing influence to the barbaric, primitive peoples of Earth. Ancient Greek legend records the mysterious Telchines, scaly creatures, half man, half fish, who inhabited the island of Rhodes, and they were described by Greek historian Diodorus Siculus as 'the discoverers of certain arts and introducers of other things which are useful for the life of Mankind'. The Telchines are portrayed as submarine visitors from the depths of the oceans, with the heads of dogs and the scales of fish over their bodies.

Babylonian myth records the arrival of Annedoti, the Repulsive Ones, who were also fish-men. Their leader was Oannes, who hatched from a giant egg and who instructed the Babylonians 'in everything which would tend to soften manners and humanize mankind'.

These Greek and Babylonian descriptions all tally with the pictures painted by the Dogon tribe. Even eminent evolution experts agree that back in the mists of the dawn of time, all human life evolved from amphibious creatures who first crawled on to dry land out of the primeval oceans. But only the Dogon insist that the fish creatures who gave them their mysterious scientific knowledge came from outer space. And only the Dogon pinpoint the precise location of the origin of their visitors, an unknown planet orbiting an unknown red dwarf star in the cluster around Sirius.

Is it just fanciful legend? Or is there another hidden star circling silently round Sirius? Could powerful orbiting space telescopes trained on the Sirius cluster discover this hidden star and its unknown planet within the next few years? And what would be the reaction of sceptical scientists to the primitive Dogon tribespeople, who would simply shrug and say: 'We told you so'?

Acupuncture

Carrying out complex surgery is one of the most daunting challenges facing modern medical science. Surgeons must be knowledgeable about the innermost workings of the human frame, and skilled with the tools which allow them to explore and repair the organs of the body, cutting and stitching, amputating or transplanting.

In the team of experts who must all use their skills to carry out a successful operation, the anaesthetists are key members. Their job is to hold the patient in a dangerous limbo between consciousness and death, keeping them sedated only to the level where the patient's own vital body responses do not collapse completely, while preventing the patient from becoming alert enough to experience the pain and anguish which could result in fatal shock. Even with the most skilful techniques, a prolonged operation can lead to serious physical damage, and anaesthetists must employ every resource at their command, including powerful drugs and numbing gases.

Or must they?

Thousands of doctors find no need to keep their patients deeply unconscious, even during the most serious and lengthy periods of surgery. On the

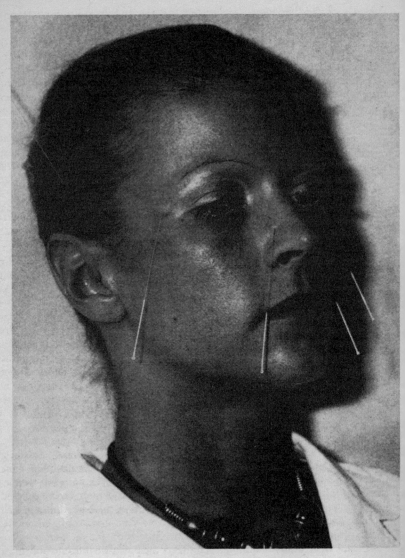

An addicted smoker undergoes acupuncture treatment.

contrary, they prefer their patients alert and able to respond to requests and give directions to the doctors – even while their bodies are in the middle of delicate and bloody operations. These doctors are the practitioners of acupuncture, an ancient and mysterious medical art where simple treatment with needles, barely pushed into the skin, seems able to effect astonishing recoveries. Acupuncture has been known to cure serious illnesses and harmful drug addictions, and can even induce a harmless state of painlessness where surgery can be performed on a patient who is wide awake without them feeling any discomfort.

For doctors who are trained to accept that illnesses usually have organic causes, acupuncture is a baffling enigma. But to ancient and modern Chinese healers, acupuncture is a simple matter of manipulating and balancing vital life forces inside the body. The technique, known to the Orient as chen-ts'u, or 'needle stab', has been practised for about 5,000 years. Before the days of refined metals, doctors were forced to use the simple tools of needles of flint, bone and bamboo. According to ancient legend, Chinese doctors stumbled accidentally on the secrets of acupuncture when they noticed that soldiers superficially wounded with bamboo arrows sometimes recovered later from serious illnesses located in other parts of their body, far removed from the site of the arrow injury. By studying case histories they slowly began to map out 'channels' under the skin where they believed vital forces controlling the health of the body flowed through key points. Translating this work into a great written medical reference book took nearly 1,500 years, finally producing the comprehensive *Yellow Emperor's Book of Internal Medicine*, carefully transcribed in 1,000 BC.

The book consists of 34 volumes of a lengthy dialogue between the Emperor Huangti and his chief physician Ch'i Pai, summing up their knowledge of the causes and treatment of diseases. The treatise gave rise to an entire tradition of medical practise based on the belief that good health manifests itself in the life spirit, 'Chi'. Chi pervades the whole Universe as a balance of opposite and complementary forces of 'Yin and Yang'.

The Yin force is said to be a soft, shadowy, watery female power inside the body, offset by the Yang force of dry, masculine toughness. Illness, according to the Chinese health philosophy, is simply a result of imbalance in these forces. The life spirit Chi flows through humans in 12 pairs of parallel channels, or meridians, down each side of the body, with each meridian linked to a vital organ – the heart, small intestine, bladder, kidney, gall bladder, liver, lungs, colon, stomach, spleen and two 'organs', unknown to Western medicine, which control the blood circulation and temperature.

On each meridian are a number of sensitive acupuncture pressure points, or gates, which control the flow of Chi. Stimulation with a needle can increase the current of Yin or Yang until the forces are balanced and good health is restored. Continuous research by acupuncturists, who originally believed there were 365 pressure points corresponding to the number of days in the year, has now identified almost 2,000 of them.

The existence of these pressure points in the body, totally unrelated to the locations of illness or disease, is denied by most of traditional Western medical teaching. Chinese charts and tiny pottery models show a complex network of meridians running in illogical lines through the nervous and muscular systems of the body. For kidney disease the diagrams show that the insertion of a needle in the sole of the foot can produce healing effects on the kidney, the vital organ located in the small of the back.

There are more than a dozen hidden pressure points on the heart meridian, which runs from the chest to the finger tips, each one a 'spirit gate' which can cure heart disorders with a needle forced gently into the correct point. Heart Point number 7, for instance, is one of the cluster of points near the pulses of the wrist, and treatment there, according to the specialists, can cure an irregular heart beat and even overcome fearful apprehension, ranging from stage fright to whimpering cowardice.

Sometimes, where simple needle treatment is not enough, a more progressive form of acupuncture is used where the ends of the needles furthest from the puncture entry in the skin are tipped with tiny blobs of burning herbs. These, it is claimed, transmit additional healing force into the meridian. An even more modern technique links the needles to power generators to shoot small pulses of low voltage electricity into the meridians.

Conventional medical authorities have tried hard to dismiss acupuncture as a quack pseudo-science which only produces beneficial results on gullible patients who are cured simply due to a strong psychological belief that the treatment is of some benefit. However, this ignores the fact that veterinary surgeons who have practised acupuncture on unbiased animal patients have produced astonishing cures. These range from racehorses afflicted with ripped muscles and tendons to pet dogs suffering from paralysis and bone disease.

The ancient textbooks of acupuncture techniques do not confine themselves solely to treating human patients. Early acupuncture journals showed details of acupuncture points for the treatment of elephants, and were eagerly sought after by Oriental merchants who valued their jumbos as important assets in countries where they were used as beasts of burden.

Although the technique was widespread throughout the East for thousands of years, when it was introduced into Europe by French Jesuit missionaries just 300 years ago, it almost totally failed to gain any following. Then, in 1939, French diplomat and Oriental scholar Georges Soulie de Morant produced a five-volume reference work of acupuncture methods. This led to a revival of interest which has now produced in France a network of some 1,500 registered medical practitioners and ten fully-equipped public and private hospitals with their own acupuncture departments.

In its own traditional home of China, the fortunes of acupuncture have fluctuated between accepted medical practice and condemnation as an outdated primitive medicine. In 1822, the Imperial Court of the Ching Dynasty declared acupuncture as barbaric and inferior to the new science of herbal medicine, and its practice was forbidden. However, it still flourished in remote country regions and gradually gained back its popularity. But it was outlawed again in 1922, when it proved futile against the plagues of typhus and dysentery which swept through Manchuria. The plagues claimed the lives of hundreds of thousands of victims and, denouncing acupuncturists as charlatans, the Chinese leader Chiang Kai-shek banned acupuncture altogether. He then launched a programme of building western-style hospitals and doctors' surgeries, stocked with drugs and chemical medicines.

The Communist government which succeeded Chiang Kai-shek drove acupuncture even further underground, vowing they would eliminate archaic superstitious medicine practised by 'witch doctors'. Fortunately, however, the traditionalists found their fortunes revived by Chairman Mao Tse Tung, himself the son of a peasant villager, who tolerantly rehabilitated the techniques and allowed acupuncturists to practise alongside their new colleagues trained in western clinical medicine and surgery.

A breakthrough in renewed research in acupuncture proved to be the catalyst for the ancient art to gain acceptance in the eyes of many previously sceptical western specialists.

In 1959, Chinese doctors announced that they had found important new meridians. By inserting just two needles in carefully selected spots under the skin, they could provide almost total analgesia for some patients undergoing major surgery. Now, acupuncturists could take their place in modern operating theatres working alongside recognized specialists.

Although the analgesic effects were successfully produced in only ten per cent of patients, the results were formidable. There were no weakening, potentially fatal aftereffects like those produced in anaesthesia. No longer were patients drugged into the twilight world of unconsciousness. Even patients undergoing open heart surgery were able to remain fully conscious, wholly aware of their surroundings and fully able to feel scalpels and forceps entering their body, but without any experience of pain. Other patients were able to sip water and eat small amounts of food, without any discomfort, while surgeons performed operations on them.

The technique was even successful in caesarian section childbirth cases, where joyful mothers were able to see their babies from the moment of birth.

And Chinese dentists reported that they could produce total relief from pain just by the pressure of a finger on a vital meridian spot.

Between 15 and 20 per cent of all operations in China that require more than a local anaesthetic are now carried out using general acupuncture analgesia techniques. A fully equipped anaesthetist stands by, in case of emergency and so that the acupuncturist has access to modern electronic tools, such as electro-cardiograms and resuscitation machines. The techniques have more than a 75 per cent success rate, and more than 100 different types of surgical procedure have now been successfully carried out using acupuncture as a pain-killer.

Just as important is the discovery that acupuncture can make a mysterious contribution as a cure for emotional and psychiatric problems. When acupuncture is used for treatment of a physical illness, patients who enjoy clinical cures also report that they feel an improved sense of emotional well-being. Now the treatment is being prescribed as a therapy for a wide range of psychiatric troubles.

Since the heart point meridians may have success in helping a patient to overcome fear and anxiety, experiments with different pressure points appear to have the effects of altering other symptoms of harmful and stressful human behaviour. For example, acupuncture 'maps' show that the ear is a junction of pressure points governing a wide range of emotions. One French researcher, who studied ancient Egyptian treatment of sciatica by inserting needles in the ear, found he could cure cravings for drugs such as nicotine and heroin by using the same method.

The treatment has been refined even further by a Russian scientist who modified a simple office stapling machine to insert a sterilized metal pin inside the patient's ear, where it is left permanently. The staple looks like a tiny metal ornament in the ear lobe. When the addict feels overcome by desire for a forbidden drug, he can apply immediate acupuncture to himself by reaching up and waggling the staple.

The latest analytical data of modern medicine may have come up with one possible explanation for the effects of acupuncture. Research in Europe had discovered the existence of endomorphins, the natural pain-relieving drugs produced inside the brain. Endomorphins are released in response to pain signals which are transmitted through the nervous system. They have been defined as 'the brain's natural opium', producing relief from pain and a soothing emotional effect on tortured bodies.

As for the actual details of the mechanisms that produce endomorphins, we do not yet have all the facts. But perhaps, when the Emperor Huangti and his doctor Ch'i Pai first drew their own maps of the meridians of the body, they stumbled on the secret trigger points which let our bodies heal themselves.

The Nazca Indians

To the early road builders of South America, the barren plateau of Nazca, on the west coast of Peru, was something of an obstacle on the route of the plans for a highway stretching down the length of their continent. With theodolites and tripods, surveyors' maps and tape measures, they slowly forged across the featureless Nazca desert, pausing only to admire the previous efforts of ancient Inca Indians, who had seemingly attempted to plot their own way through the dusty wilderness.

Occasionally they cut across the lines of an old Incan 'path', a shallow furrow in the desert floor stretching arrow-straight into the distance, or a broken line of boulders dotted across the landscape towards the horizon. At other times they found their own route running parallel to the ancient lines. They admired their astonishing geometric regularity and the undeviating accuracy of some lines which ran straight for more than 20 miles. To the builders, the lines, etched by a civilization 2,000 years old, were plainly tracks which marked the shortest distances between long-forgotten temples and villages. Where the lines crossed the path of the Pan American Highway, being built for 20th-century traffic, the route planners filled the furrows and bulldozed away the boulders without a second thought.

By 1927, after the first thin line of a single-carriage highway had already been laid between Lima in the north and Nazca, and was stretching south towards the border of Chile and Bolivia, the Peruvian Government had acquired the machines which would dramatically cut down the laborious, time-consuming survey techniques for planning the next link in the highway. They had imported three second-hand biplanes and an aerial survey team took off to fly the length of the plateau between the Pacific Ocean and the spine of the Andes Mountains to map out the rest of the route.

Cruising at 3,000 feet above sea level, surveyor Toribio Xesspe looked down with pride on the black ribbon of tarmac as it cut across the 200 square mile plateau of Nazca. He saw quite clearly the ancient lines of Nazca, the furrows and rows of boulders, where they intersected the completed section of road. Slowly, as the landscape unfolded beneath him, he began to realize that the lines were not simply random tracks across the desert: they formed recognizable patterns.

Xesspe instructed his pilot to interrupt their journey south and ordered him, instead, to put the aircraft into a steep climbing turn over the desert.

153

When they levelled out at 6,000 feet, both men gasped in astonishment at the sight below them. In every direction, as far as the eye could see, the lines had taken on the shapes of a vast drawing board, covered with elaborate portraits of gigantic animals. There was the stark outline of a humming-bird with a wingspan of more than 200 feet, there were graphic drawings, in boulders and trenches in the dust, of a killer whale, fish and animals, insects and birds, ferocious warriors wearing crowns, and more than 100 spirals, triangles and over 13,000 perfectly straight lines. All on an unbelievably huge scale.

Until Xesspe's historic flight, the mysterious patterns of the Nazca desert had been invisible from ground level, identifiable only as ditches and cairns of rocks. Now they were clearly displayed as a giant art gallery, whose exhibits were meant to be seen only by witnesses who could hover high in the skies, thousands of feet above the desert.

The ancient Inca civilization, which had drawn the lines in the desert, had flourished in 200 BC, about the same time as the Roman Empire had been spreading its power and domination by building military roads to carry its centurions and cavalry throughout Europe. But the lines of Nazca, when viewed from the air, were obviously not tracks or roads or trade routes. The great curving sweeps of stones served only to form part of the feathered wings of enormous birds; straight lines which ran for miles across natural ditches and cracks in the desert floor suddenly ended abruptly; others, of equal length, crossed each other at carefully fixed angles, pointing to different parts of the compass.

To Xesspe and his pilot, they looked uncannily like the neatly engineered runways of the modern airport they used for their landings and take-offs. But who would have built broad runways and landing sites for aircraft on a desert in Peru in the days before the American continent had even been introduced to the wheel? And why?

The first scientist to try to unravel the mysteries of the lines of Nazca was the late Professor Paul Kosok of Long Island University, New York, who began a study of the desert patterns 12 years after their discovery. His first task, guided by aerial survey photographs, was to walk along the lines and curves with his research teams, brushing away the centuries of sand that obscured many of the designs. Then he would be able to take sharper, more accurate photographs and construct more detailed plans and diagrams.

In the roasting desert temperatures, it was a job best carried out in the cool of the early morning air. And it was after a year's toil, having only restored a few dozen clear outlines, that Kosok thought he had answered the riddle. Sweeping the blur of sand away from one of the giant 'runways' at dawn on 22 June 1940, Kosok saw the sun rise above the Andes Mountains, precisely at the far end of the line which stretched straight across the desert. It was the morning of the winter solstice in the Southern Hemisphere, when the sun, which had retreated far to the north, began the apparent journey south again to bring its warming rays sweeping back over the tropical areas of Peru.

To Kosok the answer was obvious. The lines on the desert were part of a giant astronomical calendar used by ancient Inca farmers to fix the best times each year to plant and harvest their crops.

However, Kosok was still mystified about the reason for the colossal drawings of beasts and men-like figures. Throughout the next two decades, until his death in 1959, he devoted his life to trying to understand the enigma of the lines in the Nazca desert.

For most of his research work he was joined by German-born archeology and astronomy expert Maria Reiche, who had lived and worked as a school governess in Cuzco, Peru's ancient Inca capital, since before the Second World War. Working together they plotted the paths of hundreds of the straight lines in the desert and proved, to their own satisfaction, that the individual paths catalogued not just positions of the sun during the different seasons of the year, but also the locations of stars, and even entire constellations.

Maria Reiche also solved the puzzle of how Incan peasant draughtsmen could have directed a work force of labourers over hundreds of square miles of featureless desert to dig the furrows and place the lines of boulders, whose designs could only be comprehensible from thousands of feet above. Over scores of interviews with old Indians living on the edges of the Nazca desert, she discovered that the Indians themselves had found countless examples of withered wooden pegs rammed into the dry, caked earth, left there by previous generations. Within living memory, there had been evidence of the crumpled remains of stakes which had been driven into the desert floor along the straight lines and strategic points in the curves of the animal designs. Reiche was able to prove that the ancient designers in fact worked with small scale models and enlarged them into gigantic proportions section by section in the desert. Each fragment of the model would be marked out with pegs.

While Reiche agreed with Professor Kosok that the straight lines were diagrams of the sun, moon, stars and planets, the pictures of animals and the other artistic designs, she claimed, were simply there for adornment.

Indeed, Inca culture has produced countless beautiful objects of little practical value that still survive today.

Archeologists have unearthed exquisite Incan gold jugs for carrying water, where simple clay pots could have done the job just as well, and amazing cloths woven with intricate, beautiful designs, where coarsely spun wool would have kept out the desert cold just as effectively. For the Incas believed in art and beauty for its own sake. Thus, while the straight lines were practical scientific calculating tools, the exotic designs surrounding them were to soften the sharp geometric outlines with drawings of grace and beauty.

The conclusions of Professor Kosok and Maria Reiche satisfied most of the modest intellectual curiosity about the lines of Nazca. However, there was a far more vivid and imaginative theory about their origins put forward in the 1970s by writer Erich Von Daniken, the author who intrigued millions of readers around the world with his book *Chariot of the Gods*.

Von Daniken claimed there was archeological and cultural evidence that alien astronauts, in the form of gods from outer space, had visited Earth in centuries past and left their impression on the civilizations of many races. Von Daniken himself paid a visit to Nazca and announced that the straight lines on the desert in fact formed a gigantic landing strip for space travellers to set down their spacecraft. The ancient inhabitants of Nazca may have once witnessed the landing of a space ship, he claimed, and had decided to etch out their message of welcome in the hope that the space travellers would return. The lines on the desert, only meaningful from a great altitude, had the clear invitation: 'Land here – everything is prepared for you.'

Some people took Von Daniken's theory seriously, and at least one pilot brought his light aircraft in, landing safely and taking off again from one of the 'runways'. However, more serious-minded people questioned why space voyagers, presumably travelling in high-tech space craft while crossing the cosmos, should need anything as mundane as a rough desert airstrip in order to touch down on Earth.

Later still, Jim Woodman, an American aviation consultant and business-man, came up with an intriguing, and far more credible, answer to the riddle of the Nazca desert. When he visited the site, he found a number of stone pits situated at the ends of some of the lines, which seemed to him to have been the remains of some sort of ovens. Then, on fragments of pottery, he discerned some strange drawings, which appeared to depict a globe and a type of straw canoe. It looked like an ancient Incan version of a hot-air balloon. He then found samples of cloth in Incan graves, more than 1,500 years old.

Analysis of the cloth showed that the fabric had been tightly woven, enough perhaps to hold large volumes of hot air. Piecing all the evidence together, Woodman concluded that the oven pits he had found could have been 'burning pits', which would have funnelled hot air into the cloth, forming hot-air flying craft. Woodman was convinced that the Incans had, in fact, mastered the art of hot-air ballooning, and that they had been able to soar high above the desert to admire their handiwork.

Together with members of the Miami-based International Explorers Society and an English balloon expert, Julian Nott, Woodman set out to prove his theory. Using fabric spun by local Indians and a basket woven from reeds, he and Julian Nott took off in their hot-air ballon in November 1975. Clinging precariously to the reed gondola, with Nott piloting the frail craft, their balloon, *Condor 1*, soared high over the Nazca desert. The jubilant explorers in their 'ancient Incan' flying machine were able to see, in glorious detail, the great panorama of the desert designs beneath them.

It may well have been that Jim Woodman had found the answer to the mystery of the lines of the Nazca desert.

Who knows?

Perhaps the draughtsmen and architects of the desert drawings had taken favoured guests on pleasure flights high into the atmosphere to admire from the air the astonishing designs which were a meaningless jumble of patterns to earthbound mortals.

Maybe, however, the answer to the mystery is a complex mixture of all the varying theories. The straight lines on the desert floor may have been an ingenious astronomical calendar, built under the watchful eye of surveyors who floated thousands of feet up in the air to check the progress of the work against their detailed drawings. Perhaps the geometric lines were built for Incan farmers, to be used from the practical vantage point of ground level as an agricultural diary. And, just in case they were mistaken for any kind of landing site, they were overlaid with the enormous designs of killer whales, spiders and huge fierce warriors as a warning: 'This is the work of giants, stay away! Land here at your peril!'

One day, we may know the answer for sure.

Nikola Tesla

For the young Yugoslavian inventor Nikola Tesla, America was to be the land of opportunity. When he first arrived in New York in 1884, clutching only four cents in coins as his entire assets and a few technical papers, the 28-year-old did not have to wait for long to find his first job. He was quickly snapped up by the Edison company, for whom he designed and developed the power generators for the Niagara Falls hydroelectric power plant. He also invented 24 different types of dynamos, demonstrated long range radio transmissions systems and spurned a nomination for the Nobel Prize for Physics. While his work made billions of dollars for producers and suppliers of electrical equipment based on his inventions, Tesla, once described by Lord Kelvin, President of the Royal Society, as 'a pure genius', died alone and barely financially solvent in his cheap room at the New Yorker Hotel in Manhattan in 1943. Before Tesla's body was removed to a funeral parlour, an unusual thing occurred. FBI agents ransacked his room and seized all his documents on the grounds of 'national security'.

The mysterious, moody scientist who turned his back on the chance of fame and fortune is believed to have invented an atomic beam weapon, which is only now being developed as the awesome destructive power behind the Star Wars defence system. Four years before the Wright Brothers had even struggled into the air in their first powered flying machine, Nikola Tesla had actually devised a means of destroying ballistic missiles – even though ballistic missiles were not invented for another 70 years!

Within three years the temperamental, petulant Tesla had abandoned the security of his well-paid job with Edison to set up his own rival electrics company Twelve months later he had been granted more than 30 patents.

It was the income from these inventions which allowed him to retreat to the Rocky Mountains of Colorado Springs in 1899 to carry out his most important secret experiments. Tesla had set himself the task of surrounding the entire planet with one all-encompassing energy field, using the Earth itself as a gigantic booster for his own powerful generators. He envisaged this pulsating radiation of energy carrying radio messages around the world, as well as providing a form of wireless electrical energy.

His generating station in the Rockies was built around a central laboratory which was dominated by a 200-foot metal mast, topped by a copper ball three feet in diameter. Inside the laboratory was a circular electrical coil, which carried the low voltage energy for his transmitter. A secondary coil was wrapped around the mast, which protruded into the sky. Tesla planned to tap the colossal energy reserves of the Earth itself, to increase the power from his own 10 million-volt generator.

In his initial experiments, Tesla's coils radiated so much energy that they were able to light up an array of 200 incandescent lamps at a distance of 25 miles away, simply through the force of the electrical power.

Next, he turned his attention to harnessing the power potential of the Earth. As Tesla's mast sent a pulse of high frequency radio waves bouncing of the upper atmosphere, the signals were tuned to match the frequency of the returning 'echo'. With every echo acting as an amplifier in the mast, drawing energy from the Earth, the power output grew and grew. With each pulse the

Nikola Tesla – why did the FBI seize his papers?

growing energy became more and more forceful until the copper ball erupted with fingers of fire shooting hundreds of feet into the air from the glowing mast. The sheets of electricity were accompanied by deafening crashes of noise. Tesla had succeeded in generating man-made storms of lightning.

But his research ceased abruptly. Even though he was financed from the almost bottomless coffers of the railroad magnate J P Morgan, Tesla began to withdraw again into his own secret world, working on profitless theoretical research. Hoarding his laboratory notes to himself, it was three decades before Nikola Tesla gave any hint of the astonishing new project that consumed the rest of his working life. In 1934 he described a new piece of apparatus he had developed which embodied all the principles of the Laser Light – a device which was not, in fact, to be successfully developed until 1960.

It was exactly the same scientific basis as the laser, only Tesla was talking of shooting an atomic stream an infinite distance, capable of destroying anything in its path if he chose to adapt it as a weapon of destruction.

Although Tesla never explained any details of his invention, the secrets were carefully noted in his research journals seized by the government agents in his hotel room when he died.

The spectre of Nikola Tesla was raised again in 1977, when Canadian authorities reported mysterious electrical storms and radio blackouts occurring high in the atmosphere above the Arctic regions. Experts from the Central Intelligence Agency in Washington were enlisted to try to discover the source of the energy which was causing the chaos in the skies over Canada. They reported back that they believed a Soviet military rocket base at Semipalatinsk was responsible for ripping apart the fabric of the upper atmosphere – testing an atomic beam weapon based on the research carried out by Nikola Tesla 40 years before.

If Tesla's research work had actually borne fruit, he may have developed a ray gun which could have destroyed nuclear missiles as they curved over the Earth in low orbits on their way to their targets. The trajectory for American missiles aimed at the Soviet Union would take them above the Arctic Circle.

The powerful beams which were punching holes in the radiation layers around the Earth may also be capable of causing unpredictable disturbances in weather patterns. Canadian scientist Andrew Michrowski warned: 'It is quite clear to me that the Russians are doing experiments based on Tesla's ideas and in doing so have changed the world's weather.'

Watson W Scott, Director of Operations at the Canadian Department of Communications in Ottawa, revealed bluntly: 'I have been told this could be an attempt to pinpoint the exact frequencies used by Tesla in his work. Are these experiments connected with the great drought of 1976 in Britain, or the warm weather in Greenland melting the glaciers, or the snow in Miami?'